how to
REPAIR·REFINISH
REUPHOLSTER
PICTURE FRAMING SIMPLIFIED
CANING • CANE WEBBING
QUILTING FRAME•ROPE SPRING BED

DONALD R. BRANN

NINTH PRINTING — 1982
REVISED EDITION

Published by
EASI-BILD DIRECTIONS SIMPLIFIED, INC.
Briarcliff Manor, NY 10510

Library of Congress Card #81-68677

FIRST PRINTING
© 1962

REVISED EDITIONS
1964,1966,1968,1970,
1972,1974,1976,1982

ISBN 0-87733-823-X

NOTE:
All metric dimensions are shown within 5/100 of a centimeter.

Due to the variance in quality and availability of many materials and products, always follow directions a manufacturer and/or retailer offers. Unless products are used exactly as the manufacturer specifies, its warranty can be voided. While the author mentions certain products by trade name, no endorsement or end use guarantee is implied. In every case the author suggests end uses as specified by the manufacturer prior to publication.

Since manufacturers frequently change ingredients or formula and/or introduce new and improved products, or fail to distribute in certain areas, trade names are mentioned to help the reader zero in on products of comparable quality and end use.   The Publisher

THE IMPULSE TO DO

A decision to do, and each impulse that motivates constructive activity, is like a balance wheel in a spring clock. It is constantly in motion. Every step we take offers an opportunity of going forward, back or stopping in dead center. The success of an individual, family, business or nation depends on thought, effort and how we time each endeavor.

While repairing a piece of furniture or making a picture frame may seem trivial in comparison to world events, every effort that enables us to broaden our sphere of activity indicates forward movement. Each problem we solve helps keep us in the mainstream of life. Individuals, as well as giant corporations, begin to slide down hill when action is stifled by indecision.

This book explains how to do something you have never done before. Besides providing a constructive way to use time, it helps save money while it provides release from tension.

The impulse to do is a key to eternal youth. Try and you will succeed.

Don R. Brann

TABLE OF CONTENTS

YOU TOO CAN BE AN EXPERT

Like people of every age, inanimate objects and particularly furniture need regular checkups. Any piece in constant use must be periodically examined to make certain the frame is tight, webbing strong and springs are tied in position. When those who are overweight plop, rather than lower themselves down into an upholstered chair or sofa, expect webbing or a spring to loosen. One loose spring or torn webbing and it compounds the negative.

Knowing what to look for, then doing what needs to be done lengthens its lifespan and prevents more costly damage at a later date.

At one time, repairing and reupholstering furniture, like building a rope spring bed, making picture frames or a quilting rack, was considered work for experts only. Today, thanks to the availability of needed tools, glues that work wonders, easy to install springs, padding and simplified step-by-step directions, every reader can enjoy success on their first try.

This book tells what tools, glue and material to use and sequence each is required. To become proficient, read directions through and note location of each part. Your secret to success depends on one factor — what you take apart must be replaced in the same position.

Step-by-step directions also simplify caning a chair, rush weaving, building a quilting frame that will accommodate a king size quilt, a rope spring studio bed, plus a sewing table and cabinet with a foldaway top that can be used for pattern cutting.

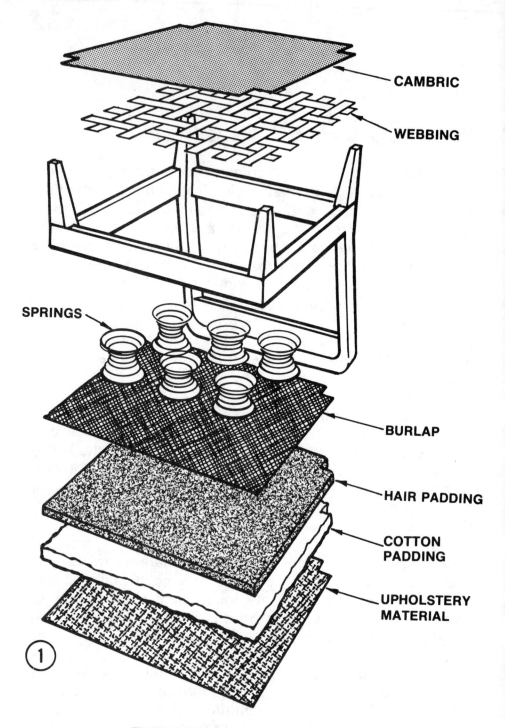

CAMBRIC

WEBBING

SPRINGS

BURLAP

HAIR PADDING

COTTON PADDING

UPHOLSTERY MATERIAL

①

FURNITURE REPAIR PAGE 16

CANING PAGE 46

③ REPLACE CHAIR WEBBING PAGE 65

(4) RUSH WEAVING PAGE 69

(5) QUILTING FRAME PAGE 79

ROPE SPRING STUDIO BED PAGE 96

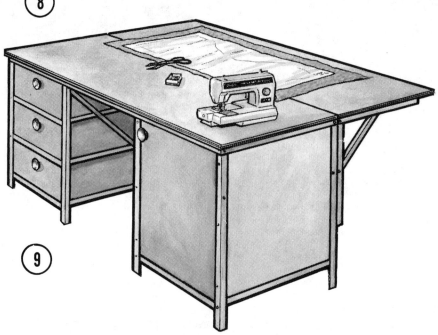

SEWING CENTER WITH LAYOUT TABLE PAGE 109

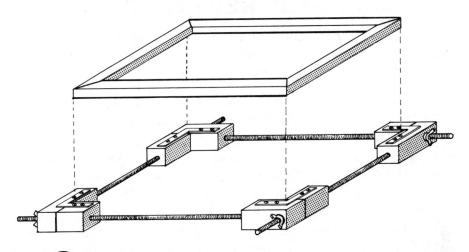

(10) Make it yourself picture frame clamp. Page 142.

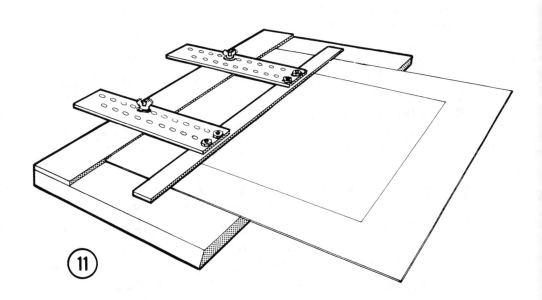

(11)

An easy to build mat cutting board. Page 148.

REPAIRING AND REUPHOLSTERING

Furniture is subjected to many stresses, strains, breakage and wear. If webbing loosens or is torn, a spring can become misplaced. This triggers much greater damage unless refastened.

The frame is also fighting a continual battle for survival. Unless a loosened joint is reglued, it, like a strained muscle, could develop into a far more serious problem. As you inspect a chair, turn it upside down and support it in position. Are the legs, seat and back firm, or do you detect a looseness? If a joint needs regluing, this can frequently be done by scraping existing glue away from edge of joint. Position the piece so a thin mixture of urea resin glue can flow into and penetrate the joint. In many cases working the loose joint back and forth while applying the glue assists penetration. Be prepared to immediately clamp the parts together after applying glue. And make certain all parts are in plumb position.

If a wood or metal corner bracket has loosened, remove it. Apply glue to joint. Dip screws in glue before refastening bracket in place. In some cases, you may have to use a slightly larger bracket and/or longer screws. Apply clamps or a rope clamp, Illus. 14, to hold parts until glue sets. Cut a piece of broom handle to tighten a rope clamp.

TOOLS REQUIRED

Illus. 12 shows the tools required when working on an upholstered piece. There are many different types of webbing stretchers available. It's essential to use one of these to tighten webbing before tacking in place.

Illus. 13 shows some of the many types of clamps that can be used to hold a frame that requires gluing. The pipe clamp is extremely versatile since it can be used to clamp any size piece. Merely use length of pipe to size needed.

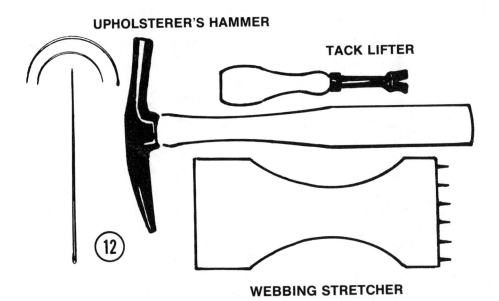

UPHOLSTERER'S HAMMER

TACK LIFTER

(12)

WEBBING STRETCHER

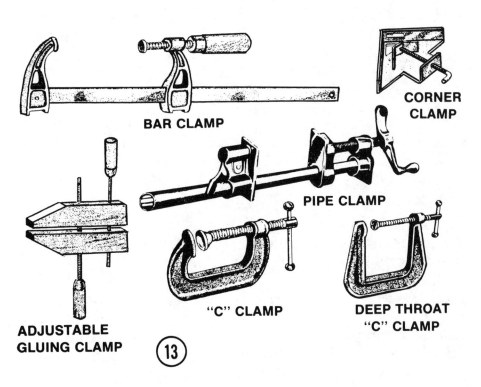

BAR CLAMP

CORNER CLAMP

PIPE CLAMP

ADJUSTABLE GLUING CLAMP

(13)

"C" CLAMP

DEEP THROAT "C" CLAMP

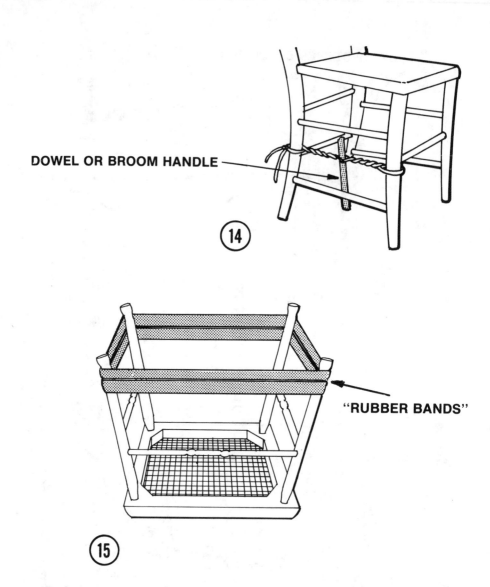

DOWEL OR BROOM HANDLE

14

"RUBBER BANDS"

15

Illus. 14 shows a simple clothes line "rope clamp" that will hold legs in position until glue sets. Use a piece of broom handle or dowel to apply needed pressure.

Illus. 15 shows a "rubber band clamp" cut from an inner tube.

After applying clamp, place chair on a level floor to make certain legs are plumb and level, then turn it bottom side up until glue sets time manufacturer specifies.

18

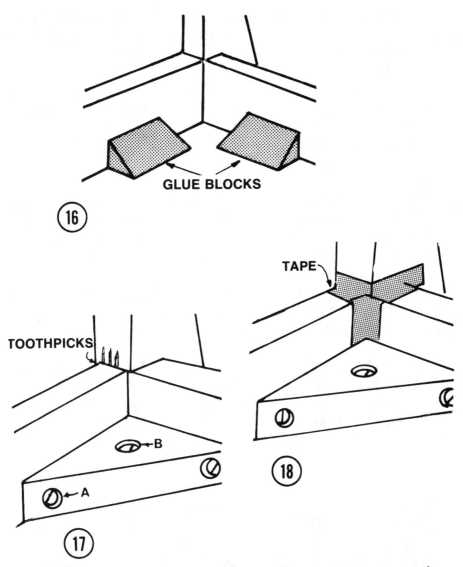

GLUE BLOCKS

(16)

TOOTHPICKS

TAPE

B

A

(17)

(18)

Glue blocks, Illus. 16,17, are frequently needed to strengthen a badly damaged joint.

If a joint has opened through misuse, after applying glue insert round toothpicks, Illus. 17.

To keep glue in joint, apply tape, Illus. 18. This permits standing chair right side up. When glue has set, remove tape and cut toothpicks flush with joint.

To make a first class repair, a loose joint should be completely taken apart. All glue should be scraped from joint. If the joint is tight fitting, use urea resin glue. If joint is loose, use waterproof glue. Always fit parts dry before applying glue to ascertain whether you have a tight or loose fitting joint. If a joint is badly damaged, study the assembled pieces to make certain you know what goes where prior to applying glue. Always position parts accurately before applying a clamp.

Allow glue to set 24 hours in 70 degree temperature or time glue manufacturer specifies at other temperatures. Waterproof glue also acts as a filler. It provides a stronger bonding agent than urea resin.

If a mortise and tenon joint is split or badly damaged, use waterproof glue or epoxy. Epoxy makes an excellent joint filler as well as the strongest possible bonding agent.

If a tenon is broken, saw off broken piece, Illus. 19. Drill holes and insert dowels. Cut dowels double the full length of the previous tenon. Drill holes the same diameter as dowel and ⅛ to ¼" deeper than length required for one half the dowel. Run a saw cut down dowel, Illus. 20. File ends to shape shown.

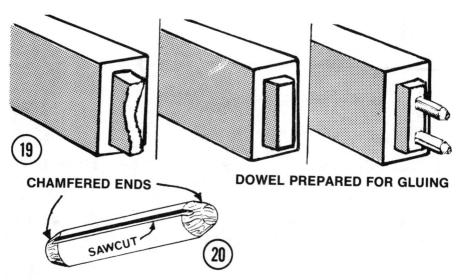

⑲

CHAMFERED ENDS

DOWEL PREPARED FOR GLUING

SAWCUT ⑳

20

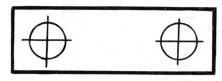

MAKE PATTERN FOR DOWELS

To accurately locate position of dowel holes, make a pattern, Illus. 21.

Use dowel that comes closest to matching size of tenon. Insert half the dowel DRY - NO GLUE into each part to make certain joint keeps parts plumb. If necessary, make dowel hole slightly larger and use epoxy or a thicker mixture of glue.

Apply glue to dowel and joint. Clamp parts together. Wipe off excess glue. Wrap masking tape around joint as previously described to prevent glue from running out when testing the furniture in upright position. Place article on a level surface to make certain parts are in place. Then carefully turn bottom side up to take the strain off glue joint and allow glue to set 24 hours or time glue manufacturer specifies.

If you don't have a clamp available, a tourniquet made with clothesline, Illus. 14, provides sufficient pressure. Tighten the line with a piece of dowel or broom handle to obtain desired pressure. Use care not to mar furniture when using a clamp or a rope.

Most glue works best in 70° temperature. For this reason, always place the article to be repaired in a room where it can warm up to room temperature prior to applying glue. Since glue only bonds effectively to basic material, it's necessary to sandpaper or scrape off old adhesive, paint or finish from area to be glued. Always wipe excess glue away from surface joint. If parts cannot be clamped, apply pressure with weight.

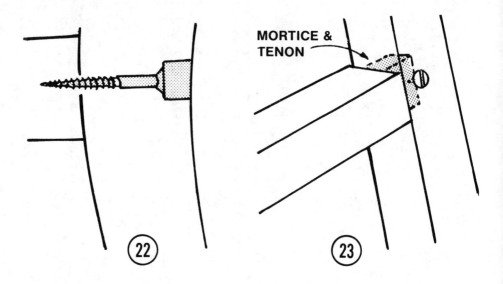

MORTICE & TENON

When taking any piece apart, be sure to mark all parts to make certain they go back in the exact position. If furniture is cracked, wedge the crack open and apply glue. Apply urea resin to a fine crack, waterproof glue to a larger one. Clamp crack together with a clamp or tourniquet. Always wipe excess glue away from surface before applying clamp.

While glue blocks, mortise and tenon joints are used on many pieces, a good many have a screw, Illus. 22,23.

It's necessary to carefully examine all parts before attempting to dismantle. Never use force.

If a mortise and tenon joint is loose, but held snugly with a brad or screw, it would be better to first try to fill the joint with a thin mixture of urea resin glue rather than remove the parts. If urea resin cannot penetrate sufficiently to do the job, you can always drive the nail or brad through with a nailset, or pull it out with pliers and start again. Use a slightly larger nail or screw when you reassemble the joint. Countersink head. After glue has set permanently, fill hole with wood filler.

Loose veneer can be replaced with white glue or urea resin.

If a leg splits, use care not to damage splintered fibers. When possible, apply waterproof glue to both parts. Press parts firmly into original position. Strap with masking tape. If the break requires more support than glue, drill a hole in the firm part of the leg and fasten with a screw, Illus. 24. Countersink screw head and after the joint has been allowed to set undisturbed for period glue manufacturer recommends, remove masking tape and fill hole with a wood plug cut from a piece of dowel, or use wood filler.

Illus. 25 shows various types of corner braces available for reinforcing furniture. Always apply glue and clamp to hold parts firmly in position before applying a metal bracket.

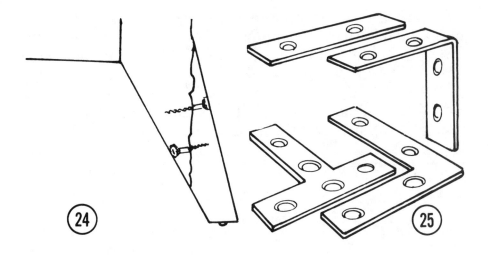

Having the right tool simplifies many jobs, helps insure better results. Always plan on working in an area where you have good light, clean space and a padded workbench top or sawhorse. A piece of old clean carpet comes in handy when making furniture repairs. There is no point in repairing a chair if it means scratching the finish. If you plan ahead and keep your tools where they can be used, it creates a desire to do many jobs you might otherwise put off doing.

The upholstery hammer is specially designed for this type of work. One head is magnetized. This permits picking up, holding and starting tacks in many hard to reach places. Use the magnetic head only to start tacks, drive tacks with the other head.

The webbing stretcher is an extremely necessary tool. It permits stretching webbing, holding it taut while applying tacks.

The claw tack lifter simplifies removing tacks. Besides pulling tacks, the tack lifter is another of those tools that helps immeasurably with many other jobs.

Two boxes of tacks help make many repairs. 7/16" No. 4 tacks are used to fasten burlap to the frame, while 11/16" No. 12 are recommended for use with webbing and as anchor nails for tying springs, etc.

Two curved needles, one 3", the other 4", and a 6" straight needle simplify sewing springs to webbing and to burlap.

Illus. 26 shows the frame of a typical dining room chair.

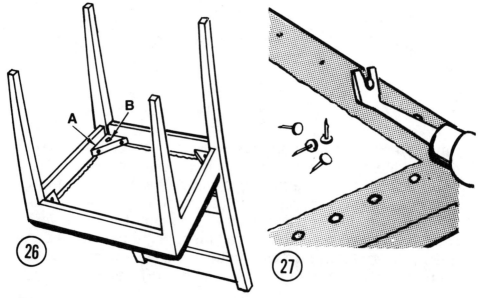

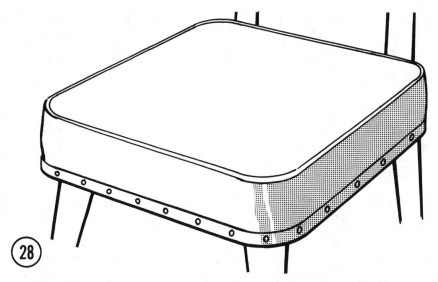

Blocks in the corner strengthen frame and hold seat in position. Screw A fastens the corner block to frame. Screw B holds seat to corner block. If a chair leg loosens, remove screws A and B. If the frame of chair is firm and you merely wish to remove the seat, loosen and remove screw B.

Make note if any screw is longer than others and replace in same hole. If a screw is loose in hole, apply glue and replace screw.

If you plan on recovering several chair seats, number each chair and seat with chalk. Also indicate position of each seat in frame.

While many seats are fastened to frame with screw B, Illus. 26, others are secured with tacks through upholstery, Illus. 27, 28.

Note thickness of existing padding so you can maintain the same height. Using a tack lifter carefully loosen and remove upholstery tacks. Remove the seat covering. Since you will want to use this covering as a pattern when cutting new material, mark the front or the back to make certain the new cover is cut to the exact shape required, and is applied in the same position.

Press old cover before using it as a pattern. Since there are many new reupholstering materials available, the simplest procedure is to use the same weight material. The same holds true for padding.

Lay new fabric face down on a clean, flat surface. Using existing material, trace and cut to size and shape required. Replace padding, retack cover in position. Always start at the middle, applying one tack to each side.

Only apply as much pressure as original material exerted on padding. Keep covering smooth, no folds or wrinkles.

Fold in corners in the same way previous material was folded. After tacking material firmly in position, replace seat in frame. Note how seat positions itself. If there are any tight places, sandpaper frame providing it doesn't show. Dip screws in glue before driving to make certain they do not loosen during the life of the new upholstery.

Most upholstered furniture can be reupholstered by following this simple procedure. You take upholstery apart, layer by layer, and reassemble by retracing each step. Most pieces are upholstered in this manner.

When you turn a piece upside down, you find the bottom covered with black cambric, Illus. 29. This is tacked to frame. Note spacing and distance from edge these tacks are driven.

Remove tacks with tack lifter. Remove cambric and you see webbing. This is also tacked to frame. Note number and size of tacks or staples used and how end of webbing is folded over and secured in place.

Next come the springs which are placed over center of webbing. These are stitched to webbing. Since springs are frequently positioned in a special arrangement to provide best possible support, always replace with same size in same position. Springs are tied together at top, back and front, side to side, then cross tied.

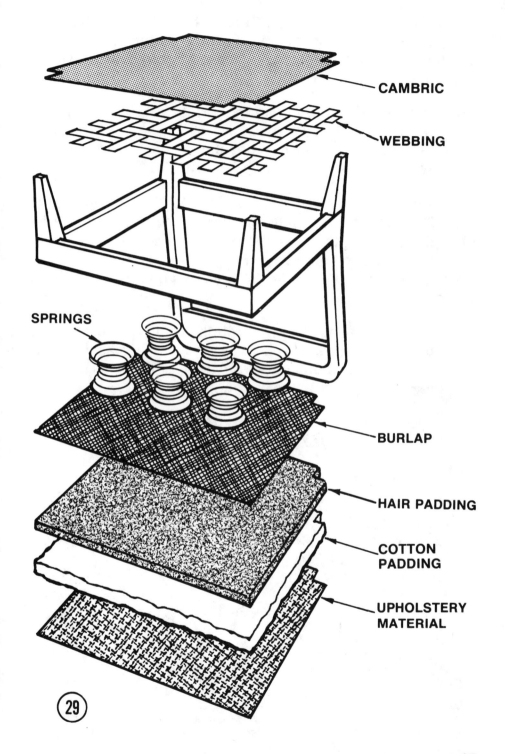

CAMBRIC

WEBBING

SPRINGS

BURLAP

HAIR PADDING

COTTON
PADDING

UPHOLSTERY
MATERIAL

29

27

Burlap covers the springs. This is tacked to frame, then stitched to springs. Next comes hair and cotton padding. The upholstery material is cut to shape required and usually tacked to frame.

There's no trick to reupholstering furniture if you note where and when each material is used. Don't trust your memory. Number each piece. Mark its position so there's no question as to which is front, back, overlap, etc.

Webbing is usually fastened with 11/16" No. 12 blue steel tacks. If a length of webbing needs replacing, cut a new one of sufficient length, Illus. 30, to use the stretcher. After stretching and nailing with four tacks, Illus. 31, cut off overage allowing 1½", Illus. 32, so it can be folded over and tacked, Illus. 33.

Push points of stretcher through webbing and apply pressure. Always space webbing same distance as webbing removed. Nail same distance from edge of frame as existing webbing, but do not use existing holes.

Webbing takes the heaviest work load so it must be tacked securely to frame. Use four tacks.

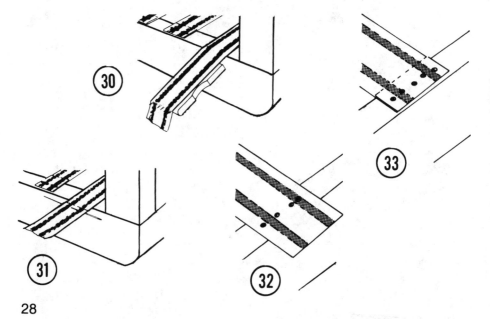

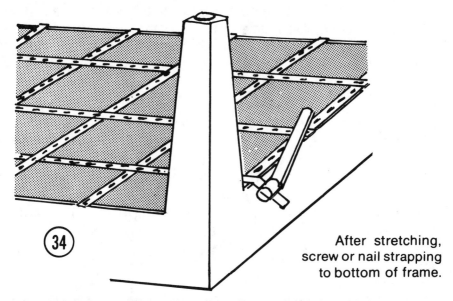

After stretching, screw or nail strapping to bottom of frame.

Many upholstering jobs merely require replacing one or two lengths of torn or loosened webbing. If a length of webbing requires replacing, remove old piece, fill old tack holes with glue or wood filler. Drive new nails or staples into solid wood.

Basket weave webbing, apply stretcher, pull tight, tack in place.

If a length of webbing is loose but still in good shape, remove tacks from one end. Stitch a length of webbing to free end with a 6" needle, Illus. 30. Pull taut with webbing stretcher. Tack in place.

If you replace old webbing, space the new webbing under the center of each spring. The cross webbing is also centered under each spring.

If most webbing is taut but a few lengths have loosened, you can, after tightening loose webbing, reinforce the entire spring assembly by adding steel plumber straps, Illus. 34. Cut these to length required. Tack to frame on one side, then use a special stretcher you can usually borrow from most upholstery retailers, pull taut and nail to the bottom of frame.

Arc nosed pliers can also be used if a helper drives tacks. Strapping can be bent up and nailed to side when side is to be covered with fabric. After stretching and screwing to bottom, strapping should be cut flush with edge of frame when side isn't covered by upholstery.

If springs are fastened to a plywood base, place one or two thicknesses of canvas or other heavy material between spring and plywood to absorb noise. Nail springs to plywood at four points.

If webbing is in good shape and the springs are securely sewn to the webbing, but the top of the chair looks as though a spring is ready to break through, start at top and work down.

Remove fabric and padding. Cut stitching holding burlap to springs. Remove burlap. At this point you will probably find broken twine holding springs at the top or a damaged spring.

If springs are in good shape and you find only broken tie strings, cut an extra length of sturdy hemp twine and retie springs exactly as step-by-step directions specify.

Always run twine through beeswax prior to using. Beeswax is available from your upholstery supply retailer. This protects the twine from rust which results from being in contact with the spring.

Much professional know-how goes into the placement of springs. Always replace a broken spring with same size and in same location. Always retie to same height as originally placed springs.

STITCH SPRINGS TO WEBBING

Illus. 35 shows how to "sew" a coil spring to webbing. Use a 4" curved needle with a double strand of mattress twine. After running twine through beeswax, knot end. Sew each spring with a lock stitch at four points and keep sewing continuously from spring to spring pulling each stitch taut. Start where indicated. Go up and over, pull tight. Repeat pattern shown.

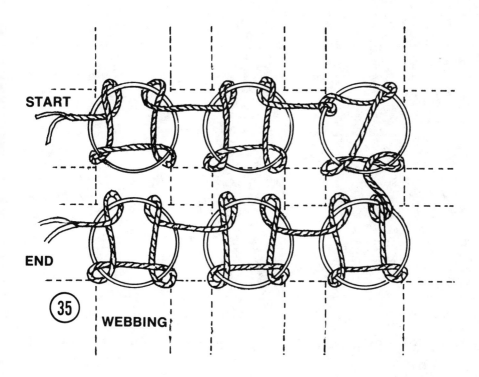

START

END

35 WEBBING

The placement of each spring and how it's stitched to webbing at bottom and securely tied at top insures the lifespan of an upholstered piece.

Step-by-step illustrations 36 to 41 show how springs are tied at top.

Measure and cut either manila or hemp twine, or use twine your upholstery retailer recommends. Allow 12" for ends A, plus overall length required, Illus. 36. Add 2" for each knot plus width of each spring and space between. After sewing springs to webbing, tie ends together, Illus. 35.

Springs are tied across center as shown, Illus. 36.

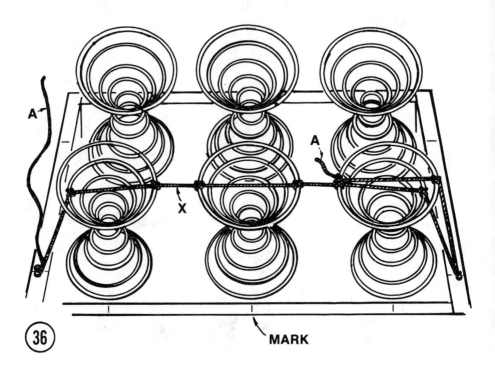

MARK

Drive two 11/16" No. 2 tacks ½" apart, Illus. 37, at center of spring. Allow 12" for end A.

After running twine through beeswax, wrap twine around tacks and tie each spring as shown, Illus. 38,39. Work from back to front, or from side to side. Locate and mark center of spring on frame, Illus. 36.

Pull each knot tight around spring and keep line taut as you fasten knot to other side of spring.

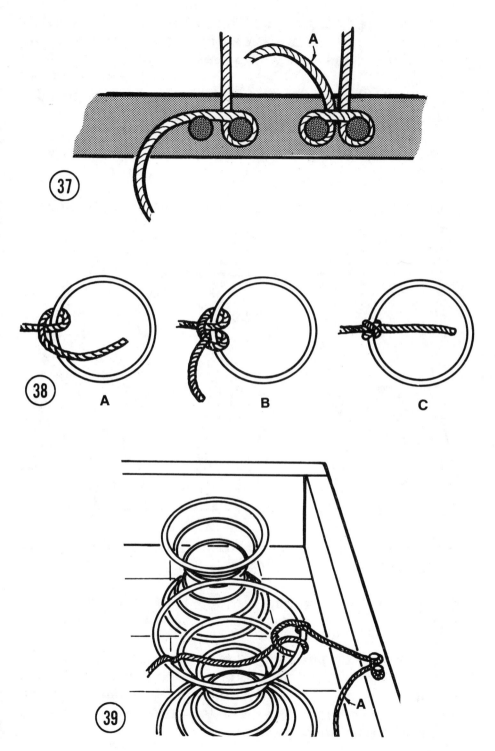

Work your way across each row. When you are ready to fasten line to other side, apply as much pressure as required to keep all springs level with others.

Retie A to both outside springs as it's shown on right side, Illus. 36.

Follow same procedure on each row, back to front, then side to side.

Cross tie each spring at center as you start tying side to side, Illus. 40.

Run twine from frame to frame between springs. Knot twine wherever it crosses, Illus. 41.

Springs may also be tied diagonally, Illus. 42. When tied diagonally, go from frame. Make a loop knot on top coil.

If you are replacing a damaged spring, compress it to height of other springs. If you are redoing a chair, measure original height of spring before cutting twine. Maintain the same height when retying. This permits cutting new upholstery material to size of old covering.

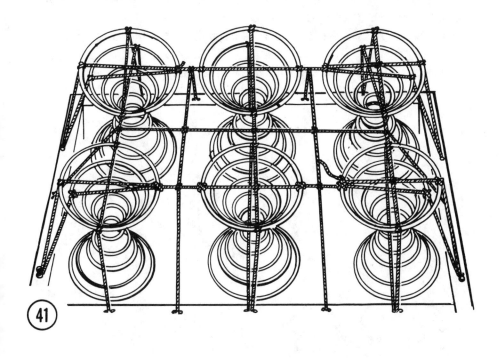

(41)

(42)

35

When all springs have been tied securely, the next step is to cover with burlap, Illus. 43. Cut to size required and tack to frame with 7/16" No. 4 tacks. Always cut burlap to size that permits folding edge under ½" or same amount as burlap removed. Drive tacks through folded edge. Space tacks 1" apart or same spacing as those removed. Do not drive tacks into holes made by tacks removed.

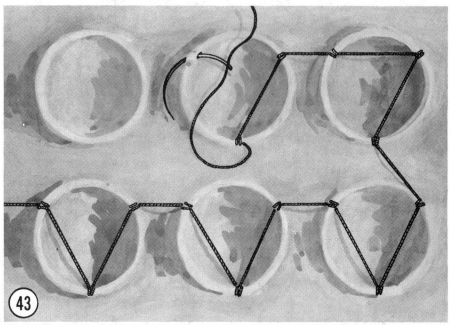

Sew burlap to springs with a double strand of mattress twine. Use a 3" curved needle. Loop each spring two or three times, at three different points, Illus. 43. Sew continuously from spring to spring.

If springs are fastened to an edge wire, Illus. 44, either tie springs to this or use metal clips, Illus. 45, available from your upholstery retailer. Position clip over coil and wire and press together using pliers.

Springs may also be tied to wire with twine, Illus. 46. Cut twine 8 to 10" long. Apply beeswax. Make loop A; pull tight. Insert one end C, between spring and wire. Wrap coil and wire two or three times. Do same on other side, then tie both ends together with a tight square knot - E.

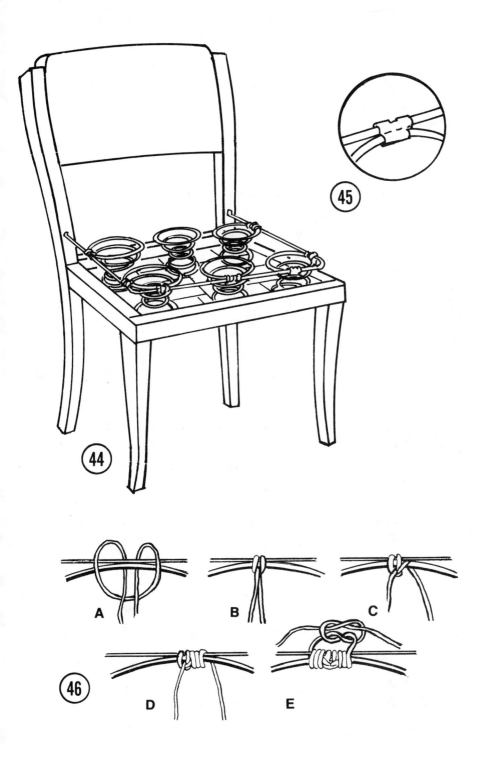

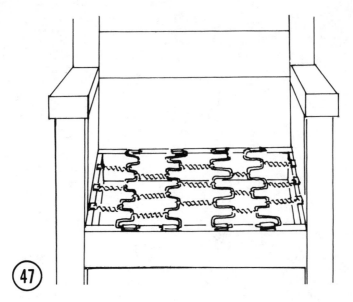

(47)

Many upholstered pieces contain No-Sag or Sagless springs, Illus. 47.

These are sold with clips, nails, helical springs and installation directions, Illus. 48.

No-Sag springs come in 12' lengths. These are cut to length required and fastened to frame with clips. Space clips 4½" apart. Cover with burlap. Cut burlap to size required and tack to frame. Foam rubber can then be used.

2½ to 3" core foam rubber is recommended on seat over No-Sag springs; 1½ to 2" core foam for back.

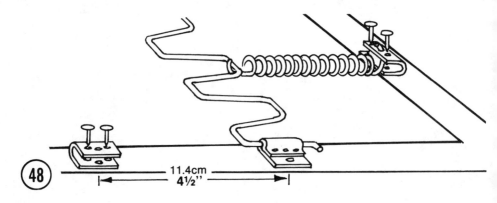

(48) |← 11.4cm →|
      4½"

Upholstery retailers offer an especially strong, wire woven burlap that can be used over conventional or No-Sag springs when additional support is desired. If you are uncertain as to amount of No-Sag springs required, measure overall size of frame and your upholstery supply retailer will recommend quantity.

An upholstered piece can be completely rebuilt by removing springs and using foam rubber over webbing or directly over ⅜" plywood, Illus. 49. Glue, screw or nail ⅜" plywood to frame. If webbing was previously fastened to bottom, fasten plywood to bottom. When plywood is used, drill ¼" holes every 3 to 4" to vent foam.

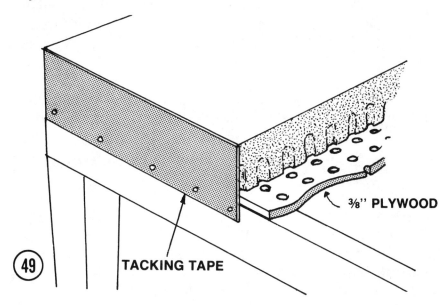

⅜" PLYWOOD

49 TACKING TAPE

Stock foam rubber comes in a slab ¼, ½, ¾, 1¼, 1½ to 2" thick; in soft, medium, firm and extra firm density. Your foam dealer can recommend density suited for each job. Always use thickness that equals padding removed. ¾ to 1½" slab stock is usually sufficient for a kitchen, dining room and chairs of similar size. ¾ to 1½" can be used over webbing while 1½ to 2" thickness is recommended over a plywood base.

Core stock is available from ¾ to 4½" thick. When redoing a seat or back where webbing is spaced 1" or further apart, cover webbing with burlap. Tack burlap to frame with 7/16" No. 4 tacks. Before cutting foam rubber, make a paper pattern to overall size of frame, plus ¼" to any measurement up to 12"; ⅜" to any measurement from 13 to 24"; ½" to 25 to 36"; ⅝" when frame measures 37 to 48"; ¾" to 49 to 60"; ⅞" to any measurement 61 to 72".

Measure full width (side to side) and full depth (front to back) when making paper pattern, then add amount indicated. For example, if overall width of frame measured 14", make pattern and cut foam 14⅜". Place foam on a clean flat surface. Lay pattern on foam and mark outline of pattern with a soft lead pencil dipped in water or use crayon. Where thin padding is required, use slab stock. Use core stock for a thick cushion.

Cut foam to shape of pattern with a sharp knife, razor or scissors. Dip scissors in water to facilitate cutting, Illus. 50.

Those who have an electric knife find this a big help in cutting thick foam.

When fastening foam over webbing or over a plywood base, follow this procedure. First fasten muslin tacking tape (available from your foam dealer) to edge of foam with rubber cement, Illus. 51. Apply cement to tape and edge of foam. Allow both to dry until they become tacky, then press together. Soapstone, available from your foam dealer, can be dusted over any cement left exposed on surface.

For a square edge cushion, apply tape to edge of cushion, Illus. 52. Tape can be applied to foam prior to or after foam has been cemented to burlap or plywood base.

When fastening foam to a seat or back covered with burlap, apply a 1" wide ribbon of rubber cement around outside

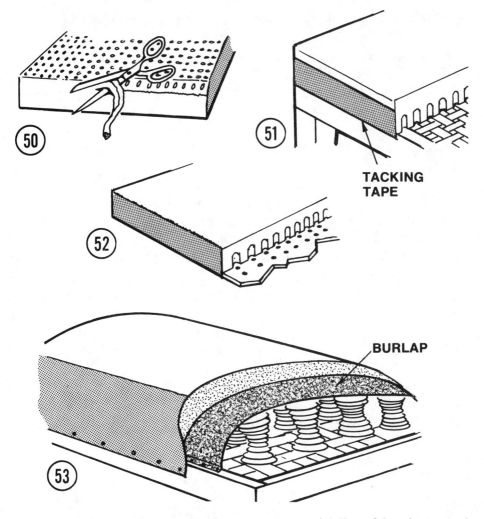

TACKING TAPE

BURLAP

edge, a large 1'' cross of cement at middle of burlap, and same to foam. Allow both to dry until tacky, then press together.

Foam can also be used in place of hair and cotton padding.

Cement tape to foam, Illus. 53. Place over burlap and tack tape to frame with 7/16'' No. 4 tacks.

When foam is used over springs, do not compress springs when fastening tape in position. Always use foam equal in thickness to hair and cotton padding.

Selected upholstery material can be lightly cemented to foam. It is not necessary to cement entire surface. Your foam retailer can advise which upholstery material should be cemented. He will also advise whether the foam cushion should be encased in muslin before applying certain upholstery material.

Always use rubber cement when applying foam to a plywood base.

For a feathered edge, cut foam to overall size required. Bevel lower edge to angle required to obtain contour desired, Illus. 54. Fasten tape to top of cushion about 1" from edge. When you draw tape down, beveled edge lies flat against base. Tack tape in place, Illus. 55.

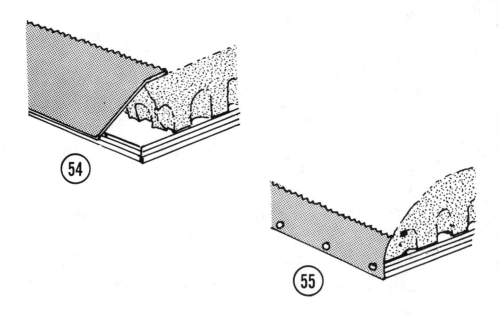

To make a round edge, Illus. 56, cut foam to overall size required plus previously recommended overage, then add ½". Bond tape to top of foam 1" from edge. Fold bottom edge under, Illus. 57, and tack tape to base making certain foam does not wrinkle.

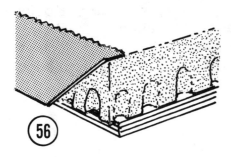

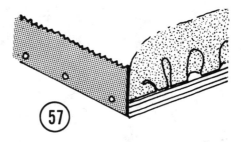

To upholster arms with foam, Illus. 58, make a square, feathered, or rounded edge following procedure previously outlined. Cement tape to edge after cutting foam to size required. Tack tape in position.

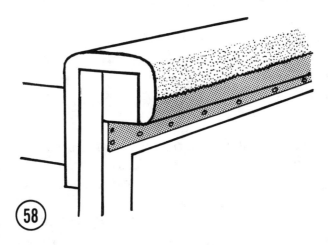

When both webbing and springs need replacing, a quick reupholstering job can be done by removing webbing, springs and old padding, and screwing 1 x 1 or 1 x 2'' cleats A, Illus. 59, to inside face of frame, flush with bottom edge.

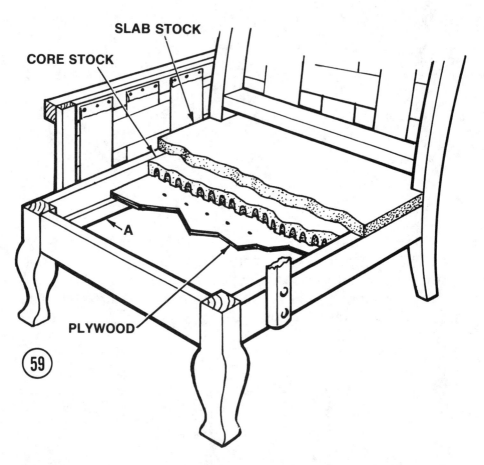

Cut a piece of ⅜'' plywood to size required. Drill ¼'' vent holes every 3 or 4''. Apply glue and screw plywood to top of cleats with 1'' No. 7 flathead wood screws.

Cut core foam to thickness required. Place in position to make certain it fits. Cut 1'' or thickness desired slab stock to overall size required. If you wish to make a rolled edge on front, cut slab oversize.

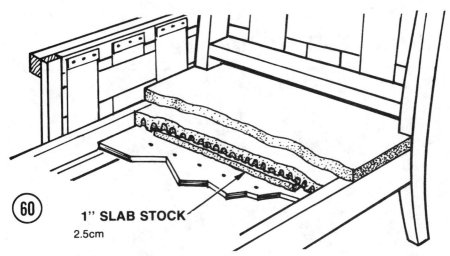

60

1" SLAB STOCK
2.5cm

If you want a crown effect, Illus. 60, cut 1" slab stock 2" less all the way around. Use 1" slab with 4" core, ¾" slab with 3" core. Cement slab to base, cement core to slab. Slab used on top can be any thickness desired. Foam can be cemented end to end to make a larger piece. Apply rubber cement to both pieces. Allow to dry until tacky, then press together.

Many upholstered pieces were covered with a muslin covering prior to application of upholstery fabric. Use existing muslin as a pattern and tack it in place. This not only strengthens and protects springs, padding and webbing, but also provides a smooth surface for covering fabric.

Cut new covering to size and shape of that removed. As with the muslin, new upholstery fabric is fastened first to back. The arms are then covered and the seat last.

Always sew in any welting or other stiffener along edge following original application. While some pieces are held in place by tacks, others are stitched. Always stretch cover to eliminate any wrinkles.

CANING SIMPLIFIED

Learning to cane a chair can prove a highly satisfactory way to invest spare time. Besides providing complete escape, relaxation and relief from tension, it proves a constructive way to build one's ego and self confidence.

Since the frame of most pieces that require recaning may also need regluing and/or refinishing, read through all directions. Study each illustration. After removing existing cane, use the awl to open all holes. Check frame to see if any joints need regluing. If necessary, refinish frame as explained on page 74.

Always select same size cane when recaning. Strand cane is sold in varying lengths from 12 to 20', in any quantity required. A hank containing 500 to 1000' costs very little.

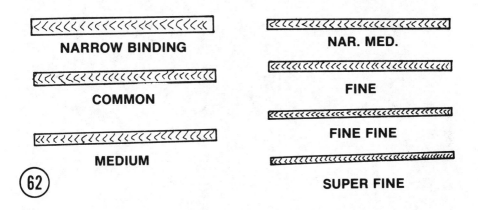

NARROW BINDING

COMMON

MEDIUM

62

NAR. MED.

FINE

FINE FINE

SUPER FINE

Illus. 62 shows the various widths that are readily available. If in doubt as to what you need, take a sample of the cane you removed.

It's important to purchase the same width and thickness as originally used. Six different sizes are generally available.

When the frame has equally spaced holes around perimeter, it can usually be recaned with one of the widths shown.

(63)

When the frame has a groove around perimeter, Illus. 63, this requires pre-woven cane webbing, Illus. 64,65, plus a reed spline, Illus. 66.

Cane webbing is available in widths ranging from 14, 16 to 18", in super fine and fine fine. In fine it's available in 12, 14, 16, 18, 20 and 22" widths.

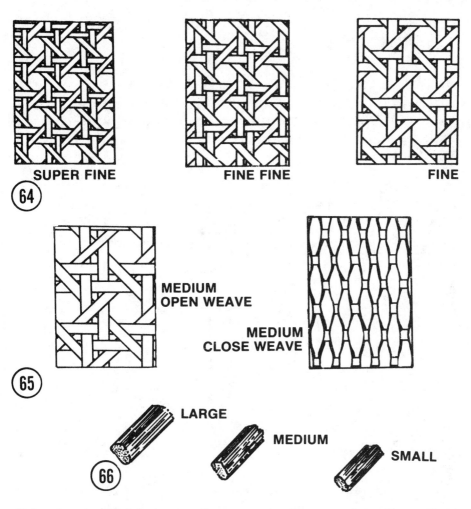

SUPER FINE   FINE FINE   FINE

(64)

MEDIUM
OPEN WEAVE

MEDIUM
CLOSE WEAVE

(65)

LARGE

MEDIUM

SMALL

(66)

It is also available in medium open weave and medium close weave, Illus. 65. Medium open weave is available in 14, 16, 20 and 22" widths. Medium close in 18" width.

Reed splines come in three sizes — small 5/32 x 3/16"; medium 3/16 x ¼"; large ¼ x 5/16". Always replace spline with size originally used.

Recaning requires using the same size material and replacing it in the original position. If you can't obtain what you need locally, write Easi-Bild Directions Simplified, Inc., Dept. 823, Briarcliff Manor, NY 10510. Enclose a self-addressed stamped envelope and we'll name a source.

TOOLS

You will need an awl, Illus. 67, and a dozen or more ¼ x 2 or 3" dowels sharpened at one end. A pencil sharpener does a good job. Use these as pegs to hold caning. You will also need a pair of cutting pliers to cut cane or heavy scissors to cut the woven cane.

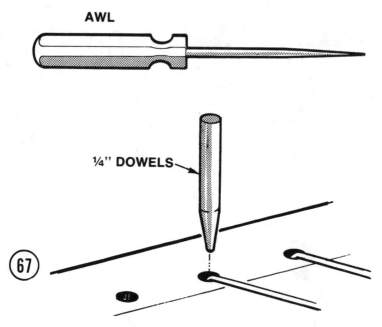

AWL

¼" DOWELS

The first step is to remove existing caning. Clean out holes and/or groove around opening. If the frame is loose or requires refinishing, now is the time to glue all joints and refinish.

Since different batches of cane usually vary in color, always order as much caning as the piece requires even if it means having a bit extra. If in doubt, measure area to be covered and your caning source can estimate amount required.

If a seat is square or rectangular, Illus. 68, it simplifies getting thoroughly familiar with the seven steps of caning. Start at rear and work toward front.

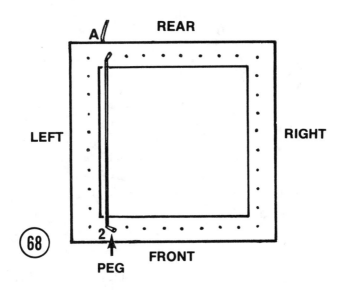

To begin, soak several strands of cane in a pan of warm water for a few minutes or as long as needed to make it pliable. Always soak additional cane just before you need it. If a strand starts to dry out while being worked, use a wet sponge dipped in warm water to keep it pliable.

Always keep shiny face of cane up.

NOTE: The four corner holes are not used until you start weaving the diagonals in course five.

Working from top down, insert cane through A, Illus. 68, allowing a 4 to 6'' end to extend below. Hold in place with a dowel.

Run cane through hole in front and peg it. You don't have to pull cane taut. Just take up slack. Never try to stretch cane. When it dries, it becomes drum tight.

Go up through next nearest hole. You can now move peg #2 to this hole. Keep moving peg as you progress. Only use a peg when you want to eliminate slack or when an end needs to be tied.

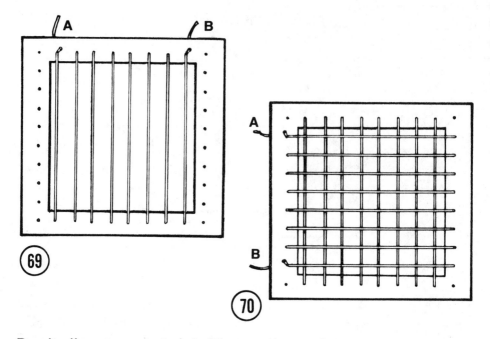

Don't allow cane to twist either on the surface or underneath. Always keep shiny side up. As the second and succeeding strands hold the previous one in place, you can use peg #2 at end, Illus. 69.

If a strand breaks, or you run out of a length, leave a 4" end through hole it belongs in and peg it. Always allow 4" to project below bottom so it can be tied later.

When you have covered the seat from rear to front, Illus. 69, peg the end.

Start the second course, Illus. 70. Proceed from left to right. Peg the first course and follow procedure previously outlined. This course lays on top of first course.

The third course, Illus. 71, starts at left front A, and works to rear. Loops on underside do not cover previously placed loops. Since you will begin to find the original pegs in the way, turn the chair over and tie each end to a loop as shown in Illus. 74.

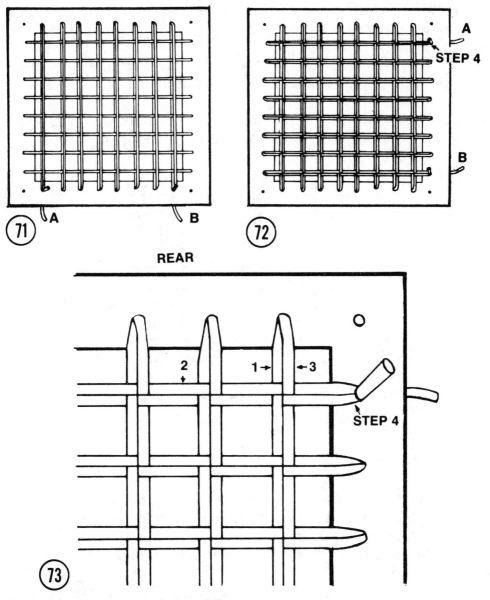

REAR

Lay this course to right of first course.

The first three courses are layers, one on top of previous course. You don't begin to weave until the fourth course.

The fourth course, Illus. 72,73, starts at A on right and works to left. This course begins weaving.

Position fourth course below second course, Illus. 73. Go over 3 and under 1.

This procedure again allows loops on bottom side to fill in between those made by previous courses.

Before removing a peg, turn chair bottom side up. Using a wet sponge, soak ends and adjacent loop until both are pliable.

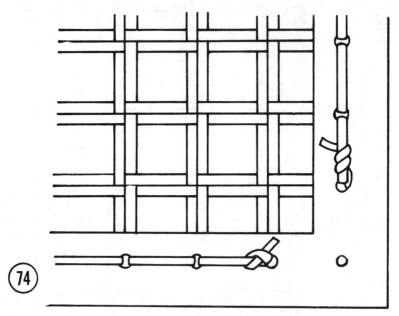

When loop is pliable, slip the awl under loop and raise only as much as needed to slip and knot end under loop, Illus. 74. Or you can wrap the end two or more times around loop. Use care so you don't break loop. When the loose end is secured, the peg can be removed. As the cane dries, it tightens the knot. If you think the knot will slip, apply a dab of white glue.

Before starting the fifth course, Illus. 75, align courses so they butt against each other, side by side. If previously woven cane has become taut and difficult to adjust, use a wet sponge to make it pliable. Start this course in corner hole in rear left hand corner. This course is woven under vertical and over horizontal courses. Peg end in place, Illus. 76.

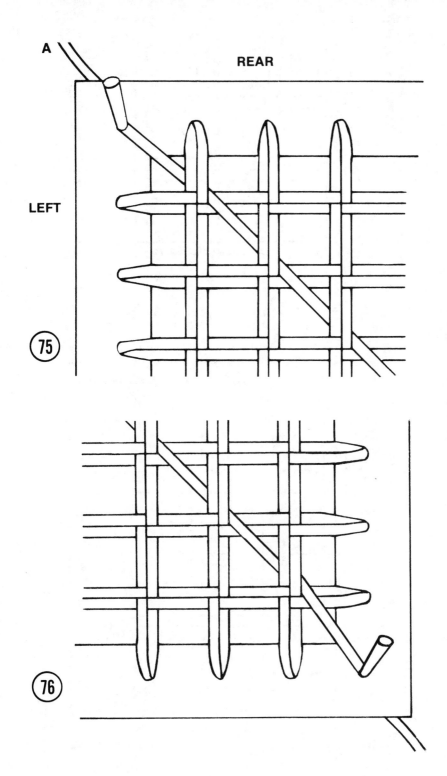

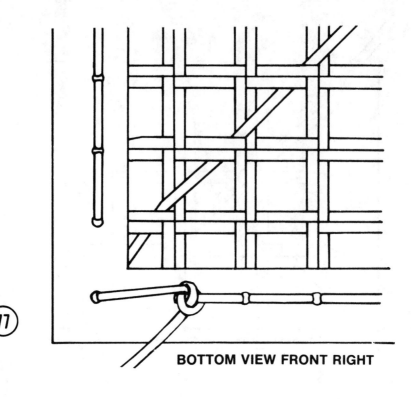

BOTTOM VIEW FRONT RIGHT

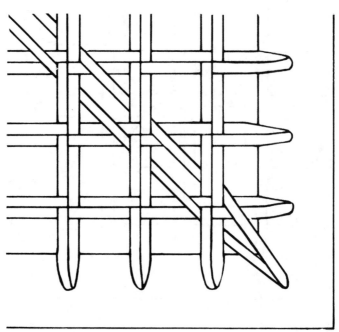

Keep this course in a straight line as shown. Aim for the right front corner hole, Illus. 76. If holes are so placed you can't go through a corner end hole, go through the hole that maintains a straight diagonal weave.

Go through corner or hole selected. Slip end under nearest loop and tie a knot. Illus. 77 shows bottom view of front right corner.

For the sixth course, go back through corner hole or hole required to achieve a straight diagonal weave as shown, Illus. 78.

If keeping a diagonal straight requires going into a hole on right side above corner hole, Illus. 79, or left side, Illus. 80, go through it. What you want to achieve is the pattern shown in Illus. 81.

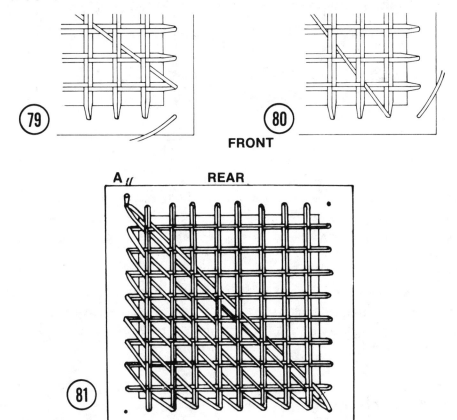

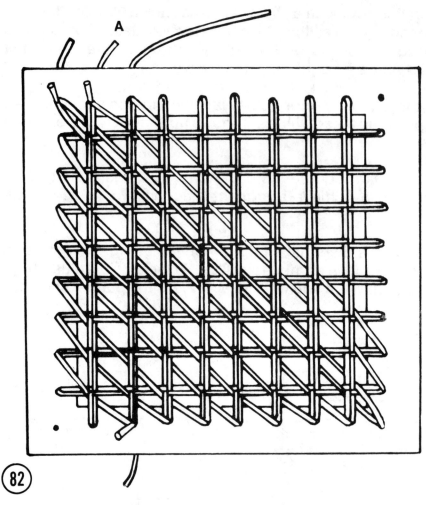

A

(82)

When you reach the upper left hole, Illus. 82, peg it. Continue weaving to achieve results shown. After finishing one half diagonally, do the other half. Start at A when doing the top half.

The sixth course, Illus. 83, starts at right rear corner hole A and works diagonally to front left corner. This repeats step five, covering lower half. On this course go over vertical course and under the horizontal courses.

Start upper half at B, Illus. 84. Soak ends to make pliable. Tie knots. Remove pegs.

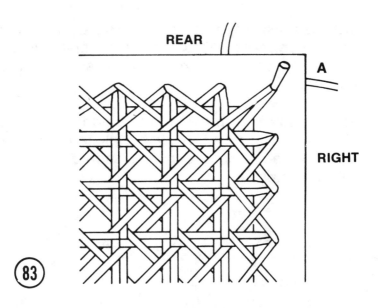

REAR

A

RIGHT

83

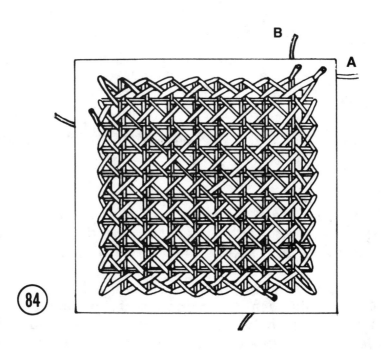

B

A

84

You are now ready to apply the binder, Illus. 85.

To bind and finish edge, use a spline, Illus. 66,85, slightly less in width than hole. Soak spline to make it pliable. If necessary, trim spline to size required using a razor blade or sharp knife.

As Illus. 85 indicates, the spline or binder, as it's frequently called, is laid over holes. A pliable piece of cane is tied at bottom. This loops up over spline and down same hole to hold binder in place.

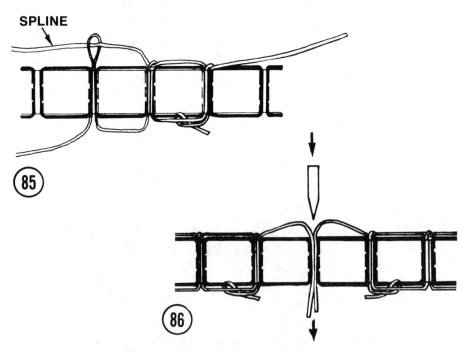

SPLINE

Allow both ends of spline to finish in same hole, Illus. 86. Fit a peg to size required. Apply glue and drive peg into hole. When in place, it should finish flush with spline.

Small holes in some chairs and oversize cane may tend to fill holes. In this case, use a sponge and warm water to make cane in hole pliable. Use the awl to make room for cane required to tie binder. Use care not to cut or crack cane or binder when securing peg in position.

CANING BACKS

Caning an irregular shaped back follows the same basic seven steps previously explained. Soak the cane to make it pliable.

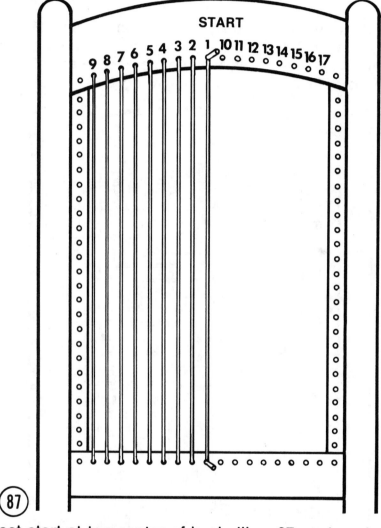

Most start at top center of back, Illus. 87, and work down. Allow a 6" end to project through center. Be sure to use a level or straight edge to make certain you keep vertical lines perpendicular and horizontal lines at right angle. Do not use corner hole until the fourth course.

To insure accuracy, number the holes, Illus. 87.

Peg end through #1 at top and bottom.

Insert peg at #10 and start with another length. Always use a sponge and warm water to keep cane pliable.

The second course is run horizontally and lays OVER first course, Illus. 88. Start at middle and work up or down, then complete other half. Always wet ends and tie same in the nearest loop. This permits removing a peg. Do not use corner hole.

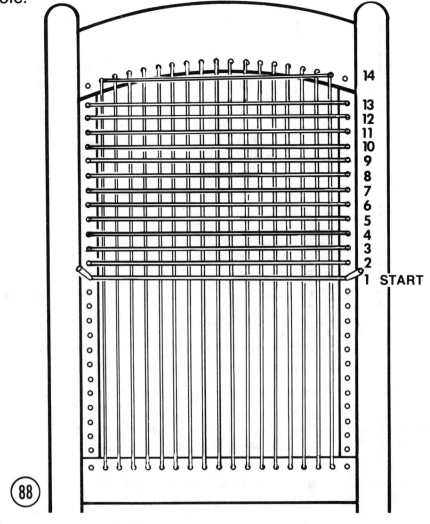

The third course is applied vertically, but start at bottom #1. This permits going through top #1 and over to #2. This fills loops between. This course lays over course #2.

The fourth course is horizontal and starts at center. This starts your weaving process. This repeats directions previously outlined. Always keep strands alongside.

The fifth step starts diagonal weaving. Start this in the corner as previously described. Go under vertical and over horizontal courses.

In the sixth step you also weave diagonally, but start at opposite corner. If in any of the diagonal weaving you find the cane binding, instead of starting by going under vertical and over horizontal, reverse the process. Go over vertical and under horizontal.

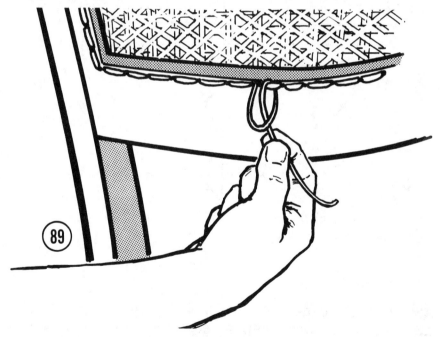

Always keep tying any ends, Illus. 89, that need to be tied.

On completion of all courses, apply binding as previously described.

CANING A ROUND OR ODD SHAPED AREA

Use a straight edge or carpenters square to ascertain exact center, Illus. 90. Start at center or as close as possible.

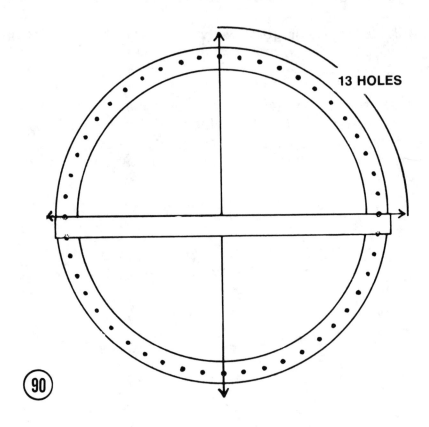

13 HOLES

90

Always install cane parallel even if you have to skip a hole or two to do it. Always keep space between strands the same size. Always check your work as you go along. If in doubt, practice with a ball of twine.

Follow same procedure as previously explained.

CANE WEBBING

Recaning with webbing requires removing existing spline, webbing and all glue from groove. Steam helps remove glue holding a spline. Only apply steam to a small area and only as much as is needed to prevent damaging finish. Be sure all glue and old spline is removed, but do not destroy groove.

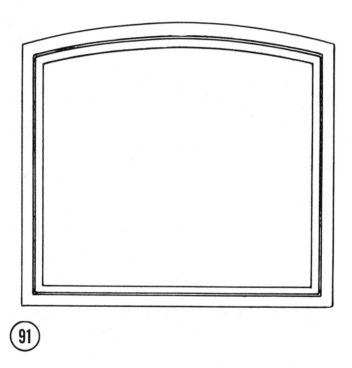

To remove webbing, experienced craftsmen apply steam then place a piece of 1 x 2 x 4" under webbing. Tapping the 1 x 2 with a hammer frees webbing. A wallpaper steamer with a narrow jet or a steam iron and a wet rag does a good job of loosening glue. Use a nailset or piece of a coat hanger to clean glue out of groove, Illus. 91.

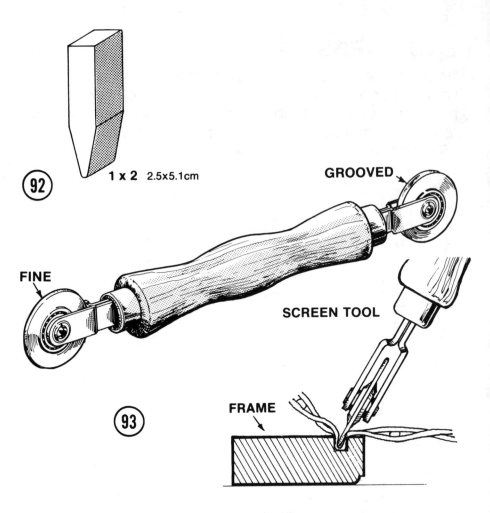

92

1 x 2 2.5x5.1cm

GROOVED

FINE

SCREEN TOOL

93

FRAME

Cut cane webbing to overall size area requires, plus about 1''
all around. Soak webbing from five to ten minutes in warm
water or until it is pliable. Place webbing in position. Bend
edges where shape of frame requires.

To press webbing in groove without breaking, make a
tamper, Illus. 92, with a rounded bottom edge. Taper tamper
to width needed to push webbing to bottom of groove. Those
who plan a part or full time job replacing cane webbing find
the groover, Illus. 93, a big help on straight runs.

While sold as a tool that simplifies installation of screening, it
works well when properly used on pliable cane webbing.

With shiny face up and positioned with equal margin all around, and with strands running parallel with the front of chair, clamp webbing in position with 1 x 2, Illus. 94.

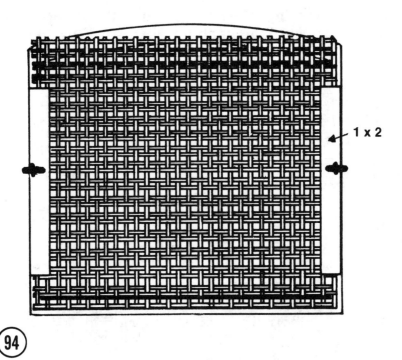

1 x 2

94

Using a mallet and tamper, gently press webbing into groove parallel to front edge. Use care not to break webbing. When you get to a curved area, use a short nosed tamper. Start by pressing webbing in center of a radius, then work out from curve in both directions.

Don't allow caning to dry. Moisten with a wet sponge. Be sure strands of webbing are parallel to frame. Take out slack, but don't apply pressure. Too much pressure will pull webbing out of shape. Remove clamp when you do a side. If you have difficulty keeping webbing in groove, cut a few wedges and insert these where needed. Use a rubber or wood mallet. Use care not to mar frame.

When webbing has been tucked into groove all the way around and strands are parallel to and at right angle to front of frame, apply glue in groove and drive spline in slot using a mallet. Apply spline in one piece. If more than one piece is needed, butt end to end until the entire groove is filled.

After glue holding spline has set, use a sharp knife or razor blade to cut surplus webbing flush with the top edge of spline.

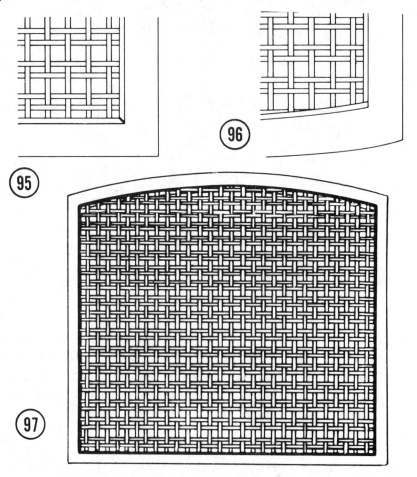

Next glue binder to top of spline, Illus. 95. Use white glue. Miter cut ends of a square shaped area, Illus. 95. Butt corners where a curved area meets a straight edge, Illus. 96, 97. Allow webbing to dry thoroughly before using chair.

RUSH WEAVING

Since natural rush is frequently hard to purchase, a handsome replacement can be made using strong kraft cord twisted to resemble rush. The average seat will require about two pounds. Two sizes are readily available. One is approximately 5/32", the other 4/32". Both are easy to work and make up into an authentic appearing rush seat.

98

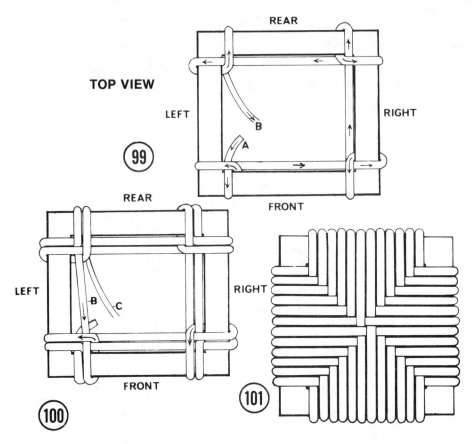

Remove old rush. Check frame to make certain there are no loose joints. Reglue joints and refinish prior to applying new seat.

The easiest way to learn rush weaving is to make a practice run using a ball of twine. Start at front left, Illus. 99. While it isn't necessary to fasten starting end A to frame, it can be tacked to the inside edge if you wish to do so.

Starting in position shown, go over left front rail, under and over A and left side rail. This locks end A in position.

Follow arrows. Go over then under right side rail, over front rail then to back rail. Go over back rail, under and over right side rail, over left side rail, over left back rail. You start the second strand with B, Illus. 100,101.

B goes over front rail and follows the same procedure as A. Take up slack on long runs as you go along. If you need to start a new strand, start it with a loop as you did at A or tack the end to inside edge of frame. C starts your third course.

Always butt each strand alongside, not over, adjacent strand. Keep all strands parallel or at right angle to frame. Tie end on bottom by looping it around the last two adjacent strands, then tie a knot. Don't bunch up the looped strands. Tuck end into woven area.

A square seat should look like Illus. 101.

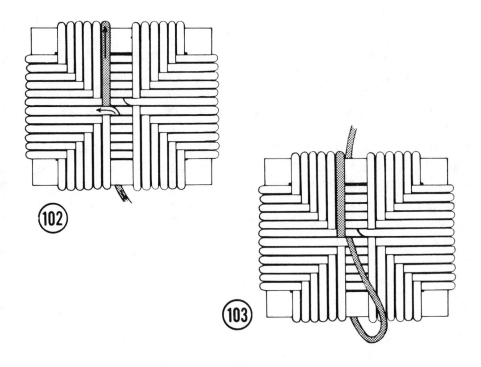

A rectangular shaped seat follows the same procedure shown in Illus. 99,100. When you have filled in the sides, Illus. 102, go over front rail and weave it under the middle strand, Illus. 103.

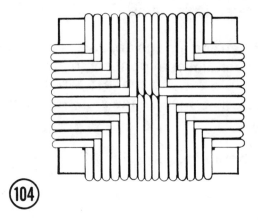

Go under and over back rail. Weave it through the middle strand, making a continuous figure eight. Continue this procedure until you have filled the space available, Illus. 104. Tie end at bottom as explained previously.

As there are different kinds of natural rushes available, fresh as well as salt water, follow retailer's suggestions concerning time to soak rush to make it pliable. Don't oversoak. Test a few pieces to see how long it should remain in the water until it becomes workable. Paint or varnish natural rush.

RUSH WEAVING — ODD SHAPE

If you have an irregular shaped seat, square it up, Illus. 105. You now have two triangles. Tack a strand at 1 and make one complete run over front rail, over left side rail, then over right rail, etc., following procedure previously outlined. Instead of going over back rail, Illus. 99, tack end to right side rail and start a new strand on left at 2, Illus. 106. End it by also nailing to right rail. Follow same procedure until triangle is filled.

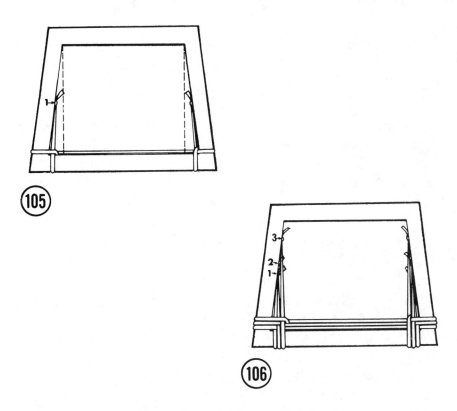

Then proceed as in Illus. 103.

NOTE: If kraft cord is used, dip into water for a minute or two following manufacturer's directions.

To pad a rush seat, crumple and stuff kraft paper between woven area as you go along.

REFINISHING FURNITURE

If you want to apply an oil finish to a piece that is covered with varnish or shellac, apply a good varnish remover following manufacturer's directions or use the new GE bromide heat lamp. If the heat lamp is used, BE SURE TO USE PROTECTIVE GOGGLES manufacturer recommends. Then scrape, scrape, scrape. Sandpaper lightly or use a medium grade finishing pad available at hardware counters.

Always use varnish and paint remover in a well ventilated area. Keep plenty of fresh air circulating and never work near an open flame. DO NOT SMOKE.

A small brush, an old toothbrush, a piece of cloth and a sharpened dowel can help remove the loosened finish from crevices and carvings. Wipe with a cloth dampened in alcohol or other cleaning agent the manufacturer of remover recommends.

Depending on the condition of the surface, always use the finest grade of sandpaper, steel wool or the new clean-up pad the job requires. Always test the grade of sandpaper on the least conspicuous area and use as light a touch as the work requires. To obtain a soft satin finish, you must start with a smooth, clean, completely dust free surface.

If a piece has any objectionable dents, holes or cracks, consider this: A dent can frequently be raised by covering it with a damp cloth and applying a hot iron. The heat tends to pull the grain back into its original shape. Always test on a piece of scrap to see how much heat is needed.

A shellac stick can be heated and used to fill a hole or crevice. This must be applied hot. A putty knife or screwdriver can be used to pack it in and smooth it over. This must also be heated. An electric soldering iron or flat iron can be used to heat tools. Allow filler to cool. Sandpaper smooth.

Always sand with the grain, not across. Never go deep into one place to eliminate a dark stain. Old finishes add a richness that's hard to duplicate.

Pine furniture doesn't require a sealer. Oak, mahogany, walnut and other so-called porous woods finish up much better when a sealer is applied. Select a sealer that complements the finish you want to achieve. If the piece is presently dark, a light wood filler will make little change. If your piece is light and you want to darken it, same can be done with a sealer or filler as many are called.

NOTE: Don't leave any rub rags around after you finish using same. Always deposit same in a steel covered garbage barrel.

Manufacturers of furniture refinishing kits usually provide finishing instructions. It's important to read these as much furniture is sold with a protective base coat.

While mahogany, oak and walnut can be finished with an oil and turpentine mixture, finishing coats containing ½ part of oil and turpentine and ½ waterproof varnish make a handsome finish. This should be buffed with a fine grade finishing sandpaper between coats.

Those who prefer a dull satin finish should use an extra fine waterproof sandpaper and soapy water as a lubricant. Sand with the grain until all bright areas are buffed off. Wipe clean with moistened cloth. Apply a paste wax and polish with a clean soft cloth.

Base coats can either consist of one part linseed oil to two parts turpentine or two parts of linseed oil to one part turpentine. The finishing coat should be mixed and applied as described. Always test on scrap lumber and apply the finish you prefer.

ANTIQUING

Hardware, home improvement and paint stores sell many different types of antiquing kits. These kits contain all the material needed to do something you have never done before.

Always remove all hardware before starting to refinish. Use coarse sandpaper to prepare surface. Remove all dust. Most finishing kits contain a base coat which is usually applied over the existing finish. If the present finish is too glossy to accept the base coat, use fine sandpaper to remove glaze.

After applying the base coat, again sand lightly with fine sandpaper. Apply finish coat. Sand with fine sandpaper or steel wool before applying the second finish coat. While one coat does a surprisingly good job, the more coats applied, the better the finish. Sand each coat lightly. Remove all dust before applying the next coat.

Most antiquing kits contain an undercoater, plus a finishing coat that is brushed on and wiped off. One or more coats can be applied to achieve the effect desired. These kits permit finishing with old world colors, pink, blue, olive, deep reds and golds.

When applying antiquing over existing paint, always remove dirt, grease, wax and polish. A solution of tri-sodium phosphate or even ammonia and warm water will cut through most wax. Always sand surface after using a cleaner. Then wipe away dust with a damp cloth.

Most antique kits provide specific directions concerning the use of all components. Follow these directions.

OIL FINISHING

Finishing furniture with linseed oil dates back to the early days of furniture making. Today it offers a good way to obtain handsome reproductions of colonial pieces at very low cost.

Furniture kits that contain pre-cut parts are easy to assemble and easy to finish. Unpainted furniture, refinished with linseed oil, provides another way to obtain what you need at a price you can afford. To obtain the exact finish you like, experiment with scrap lumber of the same species as the furniture you plan on finishing.

Mix one part linseed oil to two parts turpentine and test. Allow each coat to dry thoroughly, two days to a week depending on the weather, before applying another coat. Sandpaper surface lightly with an extra fine sandpaper. After applying three or four coats, you begin to see the finish. If one part linseed oil to two parts turpentine doesn't produce expected results, try twc parts linseed oil to one part turpentine.

While this finishing can be applied cold, it penetrates deeper and spreads better if it is applied hot. Since it is highly inflammable, use with great care. Use a double boiler and keep children, pets and all who smoke out of range.

Before applying a finish to unpainted furniture, read the manufacturer's suggested finishing directions. Unless otherwise advised, if you rub the piece down with a damp cloth, it will raise the grain. When this is sandpapered with fine sandpaper or steel wool, you begin with a smooth surface. Be sure to eliminate dust and lint before applying the first coat of finish.

Never begin to finish any furniture taken out of a cold room. Allow it to warm up to room temperature.

Hot linseed oil should be applied with a soft cloth or brush and rubbed into the surface as quickly as possible. Use extreme caution as hot linseed oil can blister the skin fast. Hot applications penetrate deep. The faster you rub it in, the better. Use a woolen cloth, burlap or even better, a piece of linen or, if available, a feed bag. If you have a feed bag, run it through the washing machine to eliminate dust and lint. When dry, it makes a great rub rag.

Since new, as well as old wood reacts to moisture, temperature and dry air, an oil finish may penetrate deep, or very little. It will dry fast or slow depending on many different conditions. When you work on a flat, previously unfinished surface, as on unpainted furniture, you have little trouble penetrating the surface. However, some graining will tend to rise under some conditions. When you experience this, allow the coat to dry thoroughly. Then rub it smooth with steel wool before applying next coat. Some wood requires rubbing with steel wool between the second and third coats. The more you rub oil in and sandpaper, the finer the finish.

When the weather is clear and dry, unpainted furniture may dry sufficiently to apply a second coat within 48 hours. During a hot, muggy spell when there's moisture in the air, an oil finish on some woods can take a week to dry thoroughly.

Never apply a second coat if the previous one is tacky. Always remove oil in a crack or corner. If a crack fills up and hardens, but is still tacky, clean it out with a piece of cloth dipped in alcohol. Use a pointed dowel to force the cloth into a corner.

An oil finish requires a lot of rubbing. The more you rub, the finer, softer and more beautiful the finish.

An oil finish is not suitable for carved pieces. It is difficult to keep the oil from building up. It is best suited for the Shaker and similar types of Colonial furniture and most unpainted pieces that have large, flat surfaces.

When applying an oil finish to the lid of a chest, leaves of a dining or fold down end table, do both sides. And always give both sides the same number of coats. This will help prevent warping.

HOW TO BUILD A QUILTING FRAME

Following step-by-step directions, you can build this quilting frame to size that permits making king size quilts.

 QUILTING FRAME

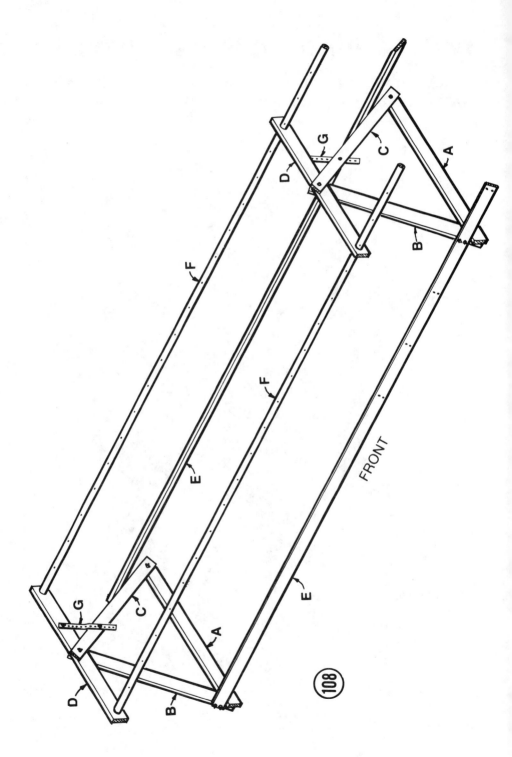

FRONT

108

80

Those who have shopped for a quilting frame usually find a flimsy one that requires costly accessories to handle large size quilts. Buying material specified not only permits building a really sturdy frame that will take up to a 114" width quilt, but equally desirable, all material costs much less than half those offered readymade.

The material listed need not be clear lumber. No. 2 with tight knots is satisfactory.

Since all parts can be taken apart for easy storage, quilting frames are very much in demand by those living in apartments as well as houses.

Everyone interested in raising funds for a church or charitable cause find an assembled frame draws many eager buyers willing to place orders.

Those who build for resale should remember many quilting frames are purchased through mail order. This adds shipping and handling costs.

LIST OF MATERIAL

2 — 1 x 3 x 12' - A,B,C,D
2 — 1 x 3 x 10' - E
2 — 1⅜" x 10'6" drapery poles - F
1 — ⅛ or 3/16 x ¾ or 1 x 20" aluminum bar stock
2 — ¼ x 3½" hanger bolts with washers and wing nuts
8 — ¼ x 2½" hanger bolts   ''   ''   ''   ''   ''
4 — 11/64 x 1½" stove bolts with 8 washers and 4 wing nuts
6 — ¼ x 2½" stove bolts with 12 washers and 6 wing nuts

Illus. 108 shows all parts. Parts A,B,C,D and E are cut from 1 x 3.

F is a stock size 1⅜" drapery pole. ⅛" holes, drilled through F, 6" from end and 6" apart, permit stitching quilt backing to pole. These poles revolve and permit rolling up the quilt as work progresses. Locking wing nuts on one end, as shown in Illus. 125, hold backing and/or finished quilt in place.

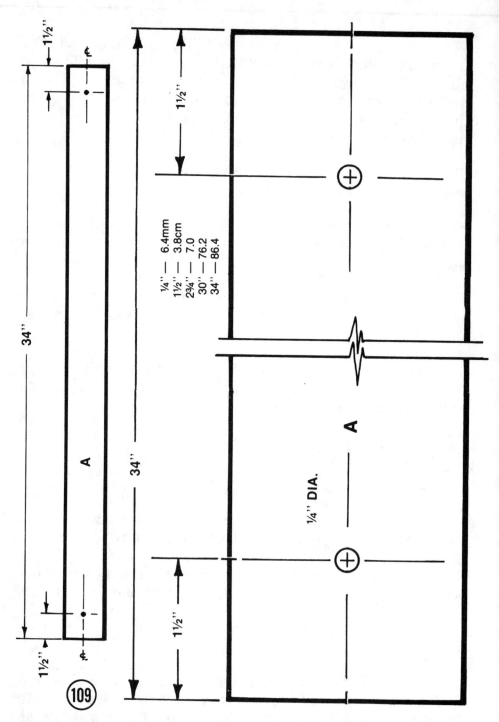

Cut two A - 1 x 3 x 34", Illus. 109. Drill ¼" hole through A, 1½" from each end as shown.

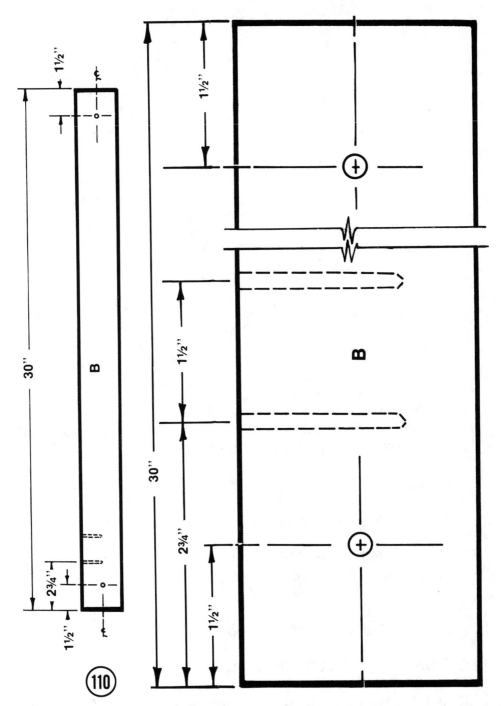

Cut two B - 1 x 3 x 30", Illus. 110. Drill ¼" hole through B, 1½" from each end.

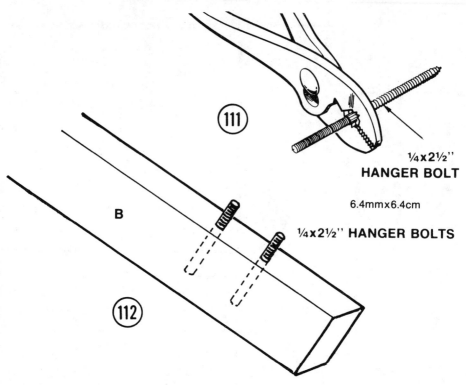

¼ x 2½''
HANGER BOLT

6.4mm x 6.4cm

¼ x 2½'' HANGER BOLTS

Place B in a vise and drill two 3/16'' holes through edge in position shown, Illus. 110. These receive the screw end of a ¼ x 2½'' hanger bolt, Illus. 111. Fasten hanger bolts in position using pliers, Illus. 112, at one end of B.

Cut two C - 1 x 3 x 34'', Illus. 113.

Drill ¼'' holes through C, 1½'' from both ends, Illus. 114.

Drill an 11/64'' hole 7'' from one end. This receives bolt holding aluminum bracing G in position, Illus. 108.

Place C in vise and drill two 3/16'' holes in edge where noted, Illus. 113. Fasten ¼ x 2½'' hanger bolts in position shown.

Cut two D - 1 x 3 x 30'', Illus. 115.

Drill 1-7/16'' or hole to size drapery pole requires, 1½'' from end of one D. This D is used on right side, Illus. 108. Note position of hole, Illus. 116.

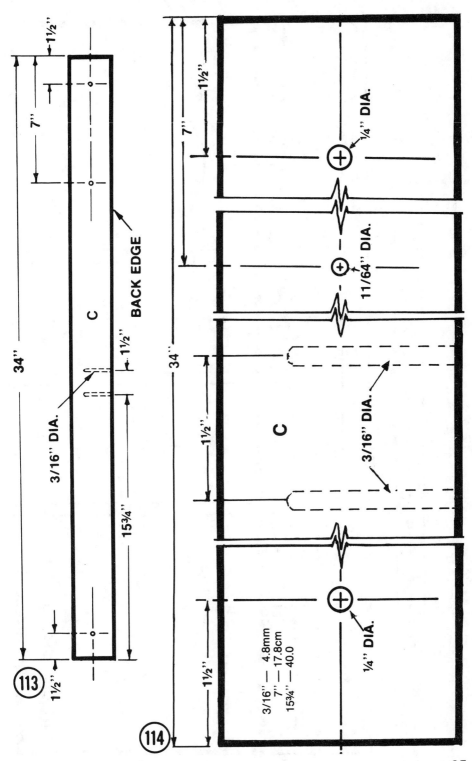

1½"

7"

34"

C

BACK EDGE

3/16" DIA.

1½"

15¾"

1½"

(113)

¼" DIA.

1½"

7"

11/64" DIA.

34"

3/16" DIA.

1½"

C

3/16" — 4.8mm
7" — 17.8cm
15¾" — 40.0

¼" DIA.

1½"

(114)

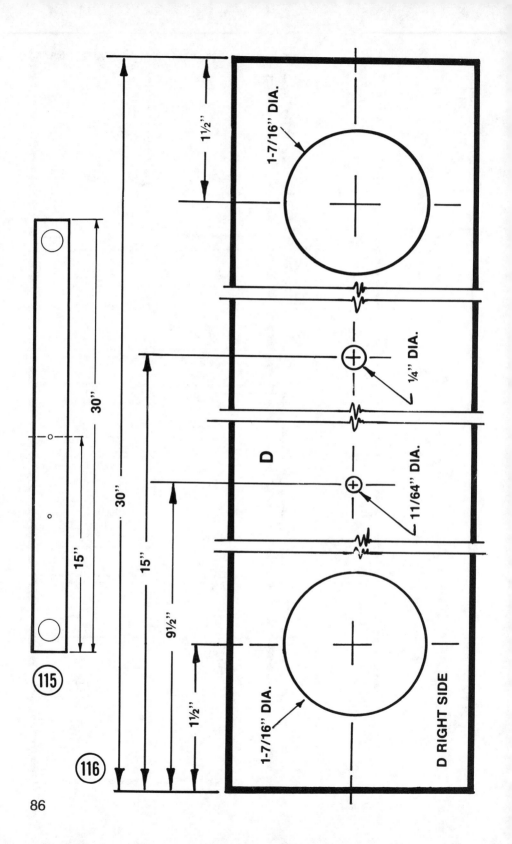

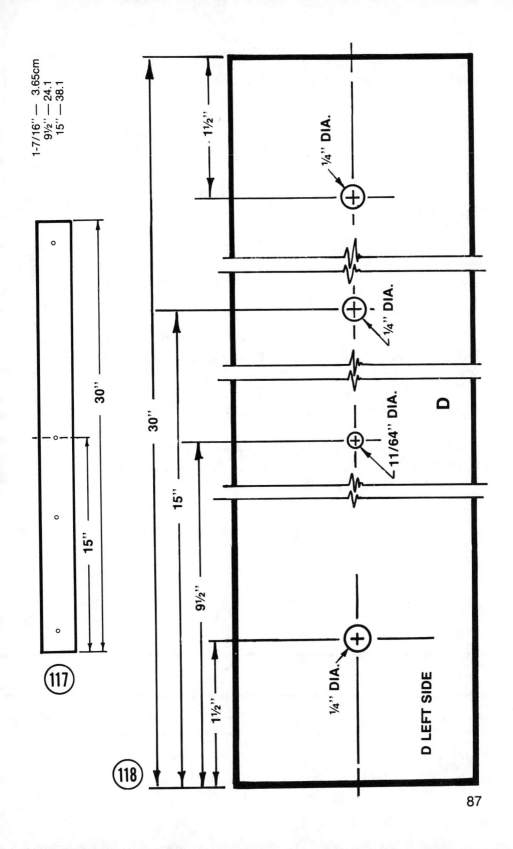

1-7/16" — 3.65cm
9½" — 24.1
15" — 38.1

¼" DIA.

¼" DIA.

11/64" DIA.

D

¼" DIA.

D LEFT SIDE

1½"

30"

30"

15"

15"

9½"

1½"

(117)

(118)

87

Drill an 11/64" hole, 9½" from end; a ¼" hole at center. Always consider yourself facing the frame when considering the right or left side.

The pole goes through hole in D on right and butts against inside face of D on left. DO NOT DRILL 1-7/16" HOLE in left D.

¼" holes in D on left receive end of hanger bolt fastened into pole, Illus. 125.

Drill three ¼" holes through D used on left, Illus. 117. One hole an 1½" from each end, the third at center, Illus. 118. Drill an 11/64" hole 9½" from one end. This receives bolt to brace G, Illus. 108,119.

After fastening ¼ x 2½" hanger bolts in BC, Illus. 119, assemble A to B, B to DC, C to A using ¼ x 2½" stove bolts, washers and wing nuts. You can also fasten G temporarily to DC. This can be adjusted to angle desired. Use 11/64 x 1½" stove bolt, washer and wing nuts.

Cut 1 x 3 x 10' for E, Illus. 120. If you want a smaller frame, cut E to length desired. Drill two ¼" holes ½" from each end, then at 12" intervals as shown.

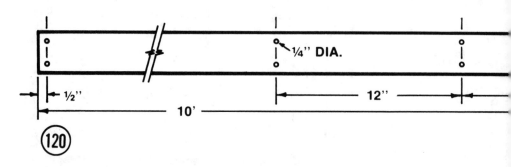

¼" DIA.

½"

10'

12"

(120)

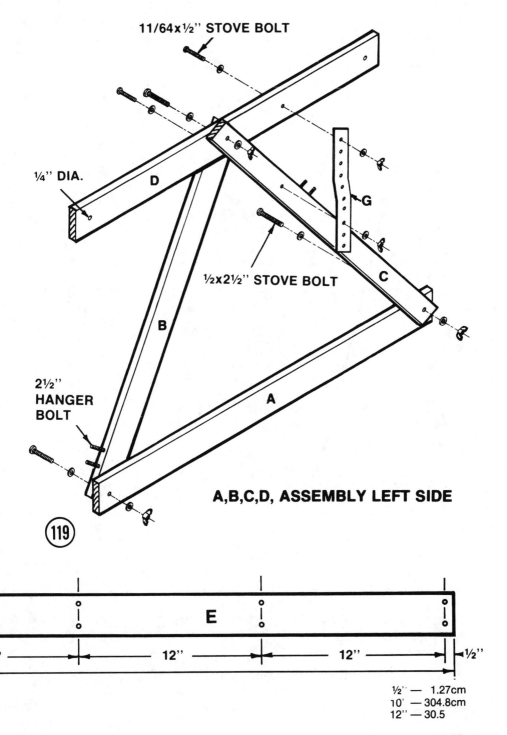

11/64x½" STOVE BOLT

¼" DIA.

D

½x2½" STOVE BOLT

B

G

C

2½"
HANGER
BOLT

A

A,B,C,D, ASSEMBLY LEFT SIDE

(119)

E

2"

12"

12"

½"

½" — 1.27cm
10' — 304.8cm
12" — 30.5

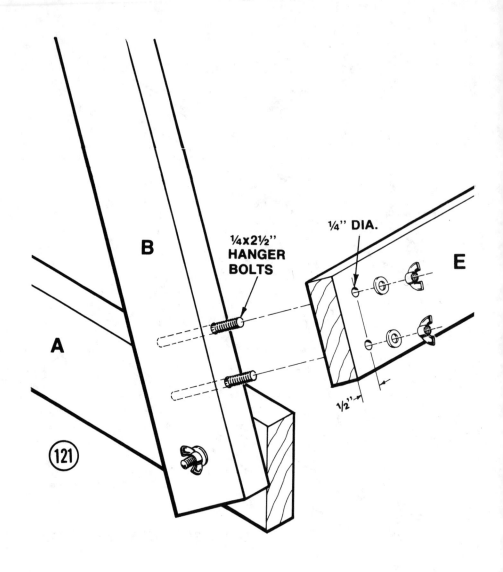

Place E over hanger bolts in B, Illus. 121. Drill holes in exact position required.

Fasten E to B, Illus. 121, with wing nuts and washers.

Assemble right hand frame, Illus. 122.

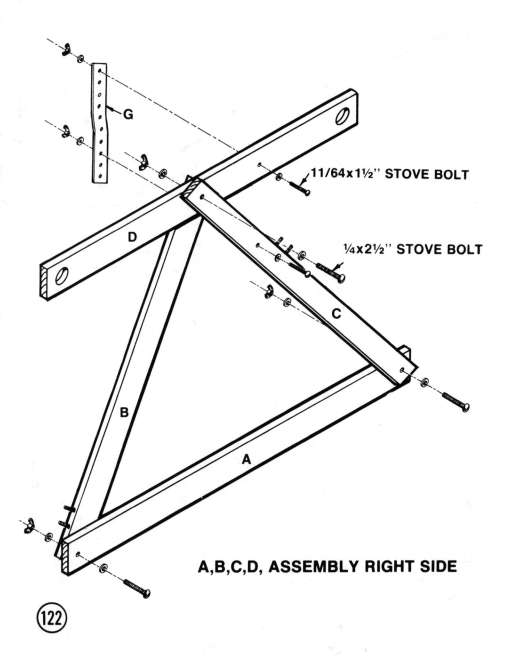

11/64x1½" STOVE BOLT

¼x2½" STOVE BOLT

G

D

C

B

A

A,B,C,D, ASSEMBLY RIGHT SIDE

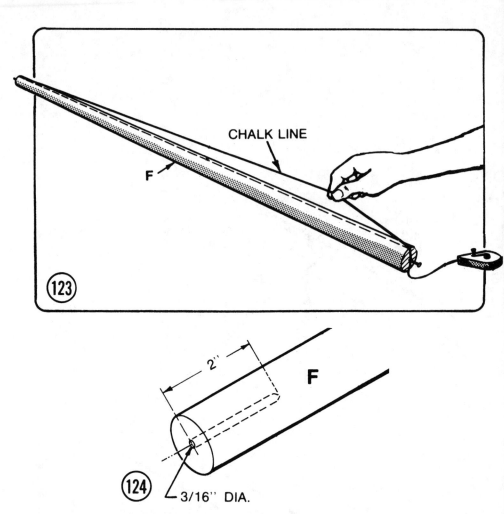

CHALK LINE

F

(123)

2"

F

(124)

3/16" DIA.

To permit stitching backing to F, drill ⅛" holes 6" apart. To keep these on line, drive a brad in center of each end and stretch a chalk line, Illus. 123. Snap chalk line, then drill holes on this line.

Drill a 3/16" hole 2" deep at center of one end of each F, Illus. 124. Screw in ¼ x 3½" hanger bolt, Illus. 125. You only do this to the end that butts against D.

Insert F through hole in D on right, insert threaded end of hanger bolt through D on left. You prevent F from turning by tightening wing nuts, Illus. 125. While a flat washer and wing nut work well, lock washers can be used if needed.

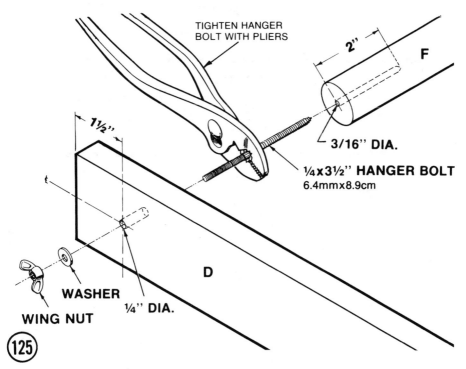

TIGHTEN HANGER
BOLT WITH PLIERS

2"

F

1½"

3/16" DIA.

¼x3½" HANGER BOLT
6.4mm×8.9cm

t

D

WASHER

WING NUT

¼" DIA.

125

Length of frame is adjusted by allowing pole F to extend through D, Illus. 126. Overall length of frame is established by brace E.

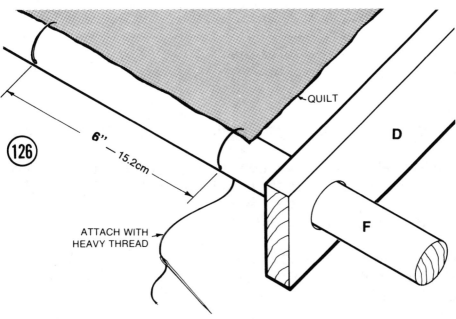

QUILT

D

6" — 15.2cm

126

ATTACH WITH
HEAVY THREAD

F

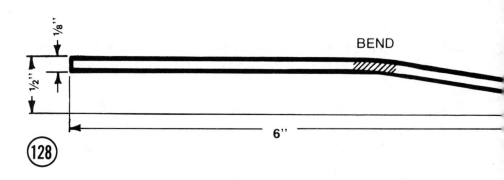

.32x2.54cm

⅛x1" ALUMINUM BAR STOCK

G (CUT TWO)

½"

1"

½"

½"   1"

10"

127

⅛"

½"

BEND

6"

128

Cut two ⅛ x 1 x 10" lengths of aluminum for G, Illus. 127,128.

Drill 11/64" holes in position shown, ½" from each end and 1" apart, center to center to full length, Illus. 127.

Bend to shape shown, Illus. 128.

G is fastened to D and C with 11/64 x ½" stove bolts, washers and wing nuts in position desired. G permits positioning D at any angle.

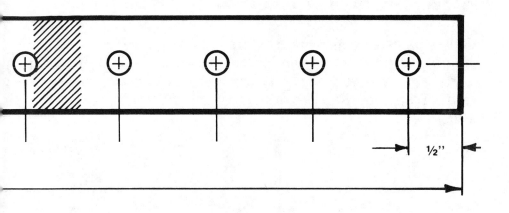

½"

BEND

Always attach quilt backing to F with a heavy thread, Illus. 126. This permits rolling up quilt as the work progresses.

When storing frame, it's only necessary to remove E and F. End frames ABCD can remain assembled.

HOW TO BUILD A STUDIO BED

Only stock size lumber and nylon cord is required to build the frame and legs for this handsome studio bed, Illus. 129. Nylon cord, strung according to simplified directions, makes a perfect spring that provides real sleeping comfort, Illus. 130,131.

(129)

(130)

(131)

LIST OF MATERIAL FOR A 29¾ x 75" FRAME

2 — 5/4 x 6 x 8' for A,B
1 — 1 x 6 x 10' for C,D
4 — 1 x 6 x 6" corner irons
16 — ¾" No. 8 flathead screws
1 — ⅜" dowel
16 — 2" No. 10 flathead screws
Approximately 230 feet of No. 3 or 3½ nylon cord

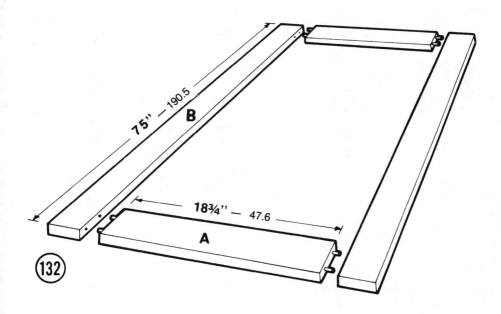

Build frame to size shown, Illus. 132, or to length and width to fit your mattress.

Cut two 5/4 x 6 x 18¾" for A; two 5/4 x 6 x 75" for B. Or cut A and B to length preferred.

Cutting A to 18¾" length permits building a frame 29¾" in width. This accommodates a 30" mattress. Those who want a frame for a 39" mattress should cut A - 27¾".

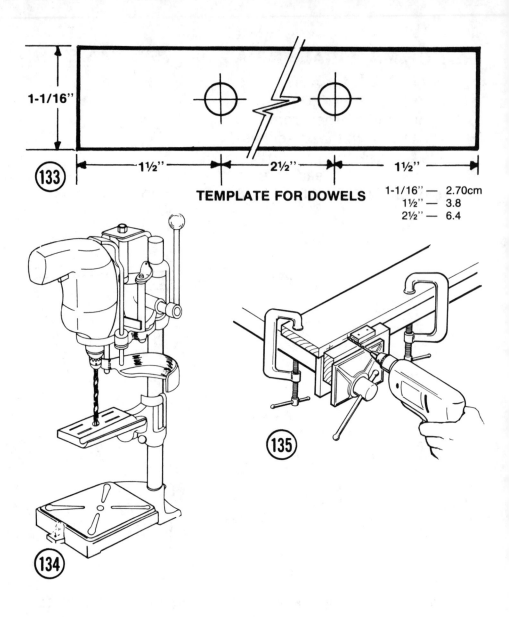

1-1/16"

1½" | **2½"** | **1½"**

TEMPLATE FOR DOWELS

1-1/16" — 2.70cm
1½" — 3.8
2½" — 6.4

(133)

(134)

(135)

Illus. 133 indicates actual spacing between dowel holes on end of A.

Position template on end. Use a nail to locate centers.

Use a square block and a clamp to hold B in position. If you don't have access to a stand or drill press, Illus. 134, make a jig, Illus. 135, to hold bit plumb.

98

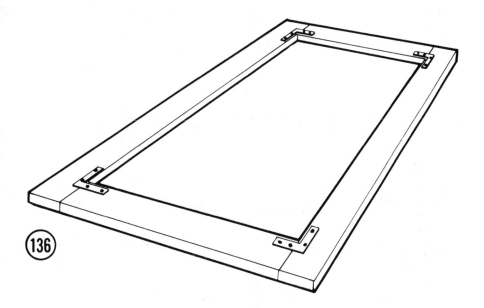

(136)

Cut eight ⅜ x 2'' dowels. File ends slightly round. Make ⅛''
deep saw cut down length of dowel, Illus. 20. Test assembling
frame dry, no glue, to make certain everything fits. Apply glue
and fasten A to B. Clamp in position. Check corners with a
square. When square, fasten 1 x 6 x 6'' flat corner irons to
bottom, Illus. 136. Allow glue to set time manufacturer
recommends before doing further work.

When glue has been allowed to set length of time
manufacturer specifies, file or sandpaper inside edge of A
and B to a bevel, to within 6'' of each corner, Illus. 137.

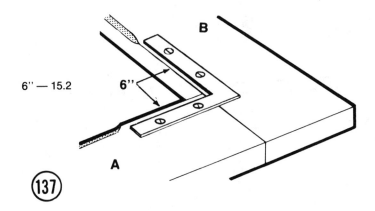

B

6'' — 15.2   6''

A

(137)

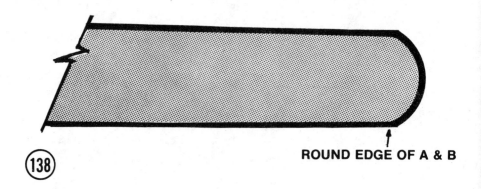

ROUND EDGE OF A & B

(138)

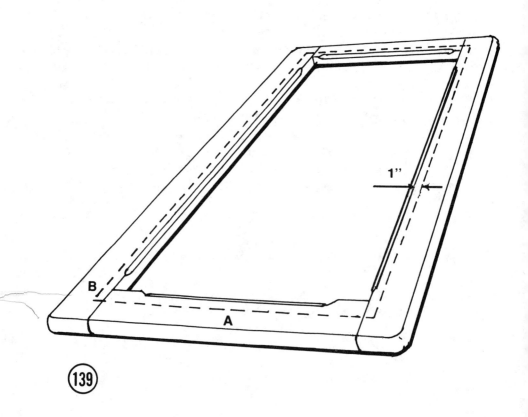

1"

B

A

(139)

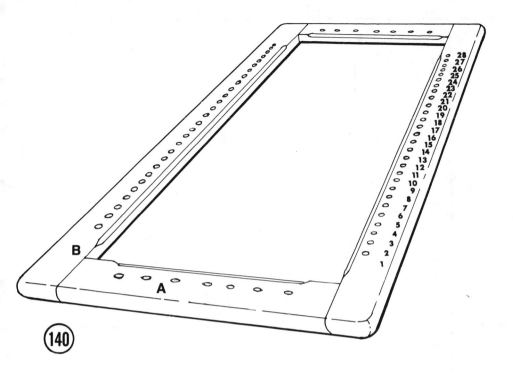

Using a file or sandpaper, round top and bottom outside edge of AB to shape shown, Illus. 138.

Draw a line 1" from edge, Illus. 139.

Locate center of A. Drill a ¼" hole at center, 1" from edge. Drill from top face down. Repeat every 2" along drawn line. For this frame you should have 7 holes in A, 28 in B, Illus. 140.

After drilling holes, sandpaper surface.

Cut four legs to full size of pattern, Illus. 141,142. Join Illus. 141 to 142 to obtain exact shape required.

Cut four legs C to full size of pattern then recut pattern and cut four legs D.

Drill two 3/32" holes in position shown, Illus. 141, in both C and D. Countersink holes to receive screws, Illus. 143.

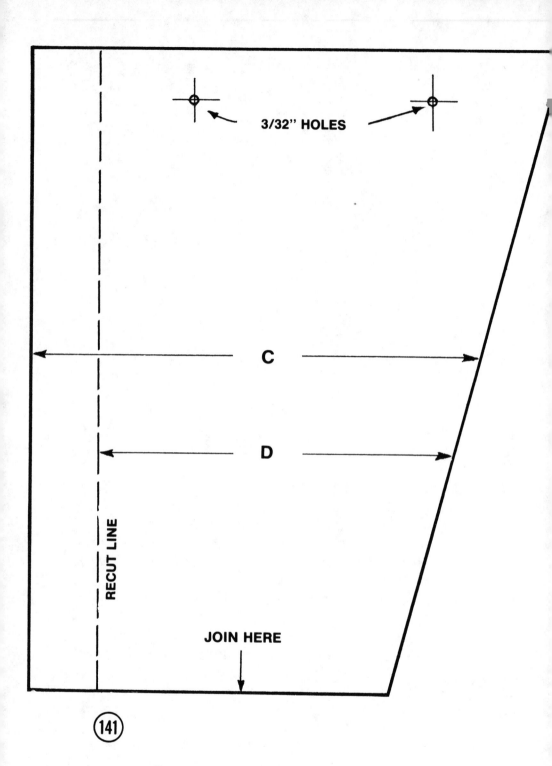

3/32" HOLES

C

D

RECUT LINE

JOIN HERE

(141)

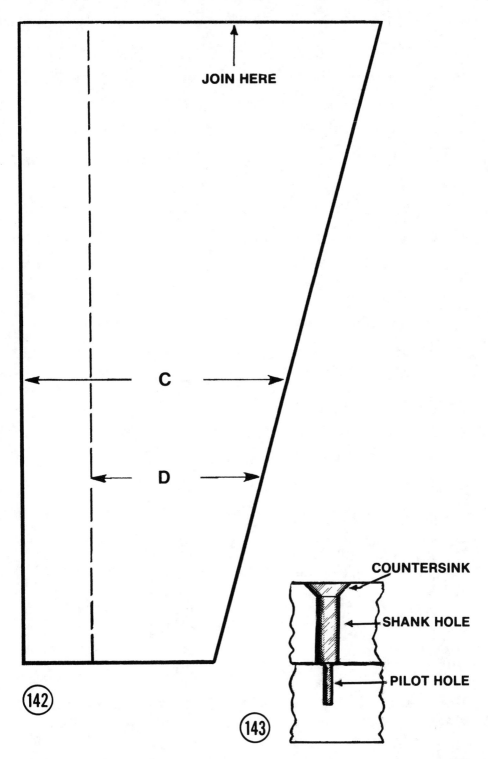

JOIN HERE

C

D

(142)

COUNTERSINK

SHANK HOLE

PILOT HOLE

(143)

103

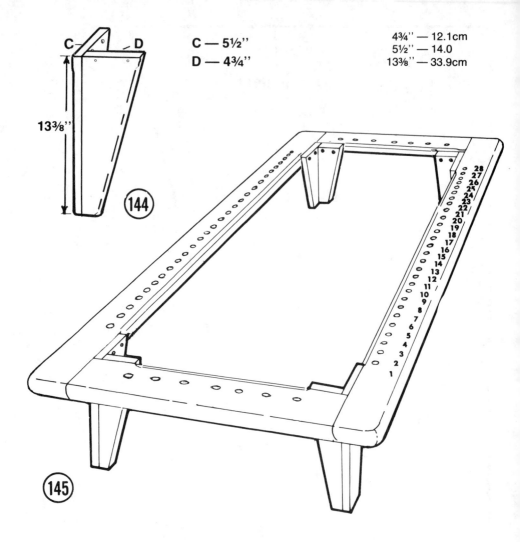

C — 5½"

D — 4¾"

4¾" — 12.1cm
5½" — 14.0
13⅜" — 33.9cm

Apply glue and nail C to D with 4 penny finishing nails, Illus. 144. Countersink heads, fill holes with wood filler.

Apply glue prior to fastening CD flush with top of AB, Illus. 145. Use four 2" No. 10 screws in each leg.

If future plans require storing frame, do not glue.

After sandpapering frame and legs with a very fine sandpaper, paint with a dull decorator black or color preferred.

WEAVING A CORD SPRING

Use a #3 or 3½ nylon or venetian blind cord for a spring. This is available in 50 and 100' hanks. Purchase 100' and roll it into a ball.

Before starting to weave, you will need a dozen or so 2 to 3" long ¼" dowels sharpened at one end, Illus. 67.

Using a match, melt end of nylon so fibers fuse. As this remains hot, allow to cool before starting.

Go up through #1 at left, over to #1 on right, up through #2 on right, down through #2 on left, etc., etc., until you reach #28, Illus. 146.

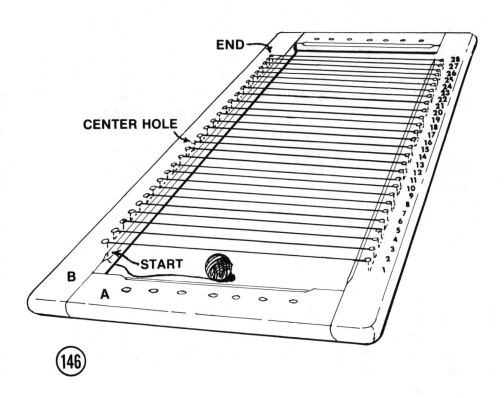

TO START OR END, USE FIGURE EIGHT AND TACK

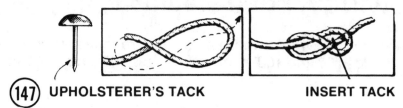

147 UPHOLSTERER'S TACK   INSERT TACK

TO JOIN ENDS, USE SQUARE KNOT

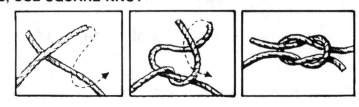

148

At this point, go back to 1 on left and make a figure eight knot, Illus. 147.

Nail knot to bottom face using an upholsterer's tack.

Take up slack in course 1 and peg it on left side. Continue taking up all slack and pegging each where needed. When you get to 28, take up slack and peg it. Cut surplus. Fuse end. Make knot and tack knot to bottom face of frame.

If you use shorter lengths of nylon, ends can be joined with a square knot, Illus. 148. Drive an upholsterer's tack through knot.

Follow same procedure when stringing second course, Illus. 149. This can start at A1 and end at 7.

Illus. 150 shows the third course.

Start at B1 at left and go diagonally through to A1. After completing the first four rows, go from B5 to B10 and do four more rows to 8 on left. Skip 9 and go up through 10 on left, back to 5 on right, and do four rows. Repeat procedure until you have covered frame, Illus. 150.

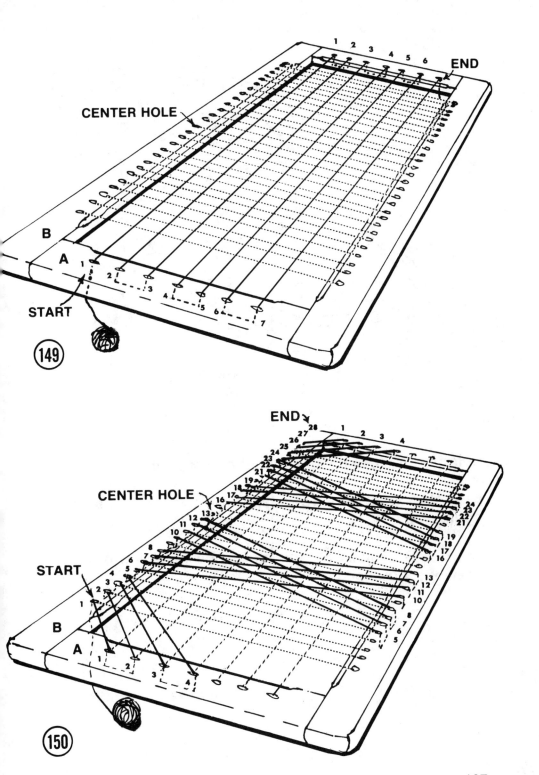

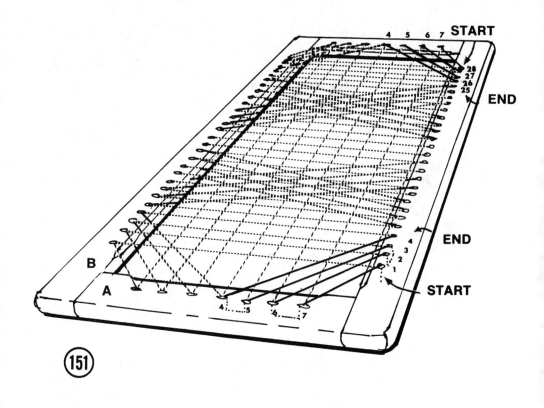

Using pegs, take up slack, knot and tack ends in place.

Next start at 28, Illus. 151. Make knot and tack end at 28 and again at 25.

Start at B1, Illus. 151 and end at B4 following procedure previously outlined.

SEWING TABLE AND CRAFTS CENTER

As the economy necessitates "making do," the extra time spent at home requires needed work areas. Reupholstering furniture and dressmaking are but two of the many areas that need a suitable place to work. This 2'0" x 6'0" desk, Illus. 152, offers a foldover top that opens up a 4'0" x 6'0" layout table, Illus. 153. Cutting fabric to a pattern, model railroading to assembling model planes is easier when you have a place to work.

(152)

(153)

Simplified step-by-step construction permits installing three large drawers on one side, a large sewing machine cabinet on other. Or drawers can be installed on both sides.

As previously suggested, to become thoroughly familiar with procedure, read directions through and note location of each part as it is mentioned.

To simplify building, the list of material specifies 1 x 1" aluminum angle for legs and framing, plywood and hardware readily available. Building it yourself saves between one half to two thirds store costs.

LIST OF MATERIAL

13 — 1 x 1" x 6' aluminum angle - A,B,C (1/16" thick)
1 — 1/8 or 1/4 x 1" x 6' aluminum bar stock - D
20 lineal feet 3/4" aluminum edging
41 — 3/16 x 1/2" alum. roundhead machine screws, hex nuts
7 — 3/16 x 3/4"   "   "   "   "   "   "
8 — 3/16 x 1/2" alum. flathead stove bolts, nuts
8 — 3/16 x 3/4"   "   "   "   "   "
14 — 3/4" No. 8 alum. panhead tapping screws
24 — 3/8" No. 6   "   "   "   "
1 box 1 1/4" brads
1/4 lb. 4d finishing nails
2 pr. 1 1/2 x 1 1/2" narrow hinges
1 — 6' and 1 — 2' length of 1 1/2" continuous hinge
    (open size) and 3/4" No. 4 flathead screws needed
1 — 3/4" x 4 x 8' plywood
1 — 3/4" x 2 x 2'   "   - cabinet shelf optional
3 — 3/8" x 4 x 4'   "
4 — 2 1/2" dia. aluminum or dull steel drawer knobs
1 — cabinet (bullet type) catch
8 — angle plate casters (optional)

Cut eight 1 x 1 x 26 1/2" aluminum angle for legs, Illus. 154. Drill 3/16" holes in location shown in four legs used for drawer framing. The rear right leg has an extra hole to accommodate brace D.

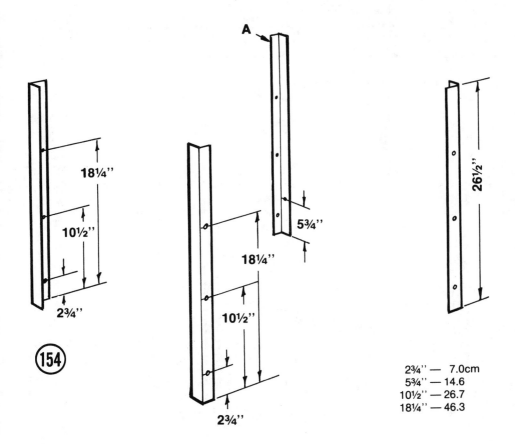

18¼"

10½"

2¾"

(154)

5¾"

18¼"

10½"

2¾"

26½"

2¾" — 7.0cm
5¾" — 14.6
10½" — 26.7
18¼" — 46.3

A

If you install drawers on both sides, drill holes in other four legs except the extra one in the right rear leg.

Cut six 1 x 1" angle 23¾" for B, Illus. 155,156. End of B butts against inside face of A. Place B against A. Using a pencil, indicate position of hole. This should be ½", plus or minus, from end depending on thickness of angle. Drill 3/16" holes.

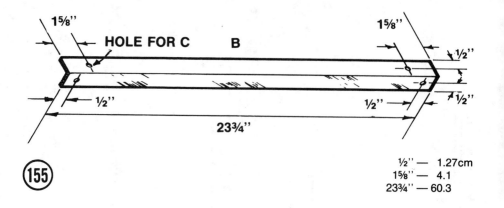

HOLE FOR C   **B**

1⅝"

1⅝"

½"

½"

½"

½"

½"

23¾"

½" — 1.27cm
1⅝" — 4.1
23¾" — 60.3

(155)

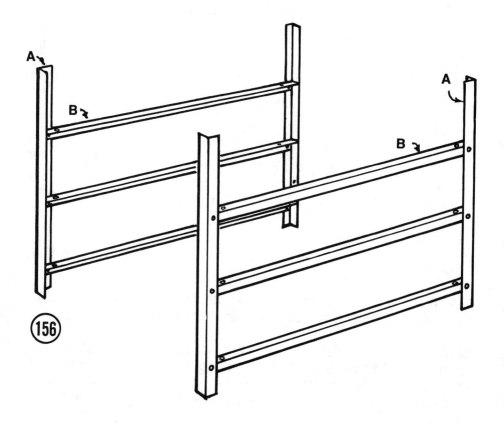

A

A

B

B

(156)

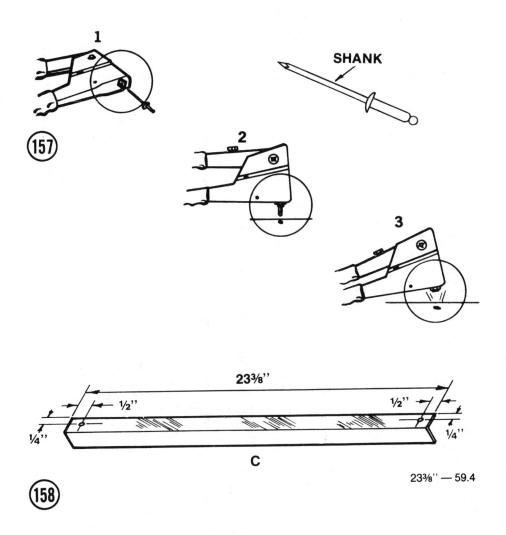

SHANK

23⅜" — 59.4

Fasten A to B with 3/16 x ½" aluminum roundhead machine screws and hex nuts. Keep head on leg. Or you can use ½" Poprivets, Illus. 157. Insert Poprivet through A into B. Insert shank in Poprivet gun. Keep pressing handle until rivet snaps off. This makes a very neat connection.

After assembling front, assemble rear frame following same procedure.

Cut six 1 x 1" angle 23⅜" for drawer glides C, Illus. 158.

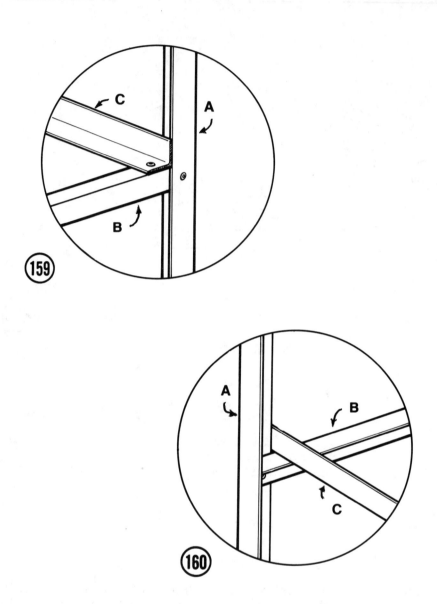

Butt C against edge of A, Illus. 159, with end finishing flush with A, Illus. 159.

Using a pencil, mark location of hole in B and drill holes through C.

Fasten C to B, Illus. 160.

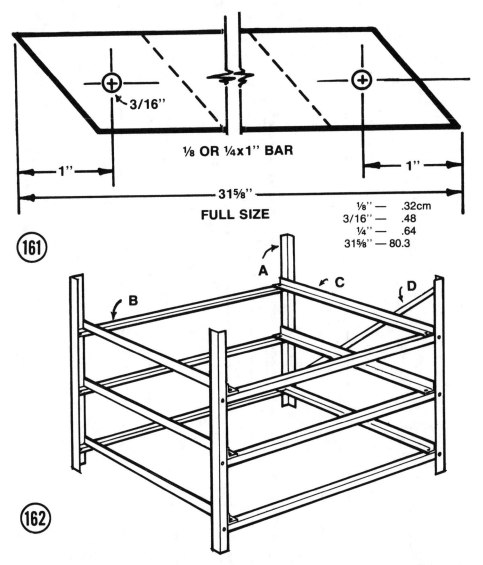

3/16"

⅛ OR ¼x1" BAR

1"

1"

31⅝"

FULL SIZE

⅛" —	.32cm
3/16" —	.48
¼" —	.64
31⅝" —	80.3

(161)

A

C

B

D

(162)

Cut ends of ¼ x 1 x 31⅝" aluminum bar stock D to angle shown full size, Illus. 161. This is used as a diagonal brace, Illus. 162.

Check leg framing to make certain it's square. Do this by measuring diagonals. When diagonals are equal, legs are considered square.

Place D in position, Illus. 162, to inside face of legs. Mark location of holes. Drill holes in leg, then fasten D in position.

115

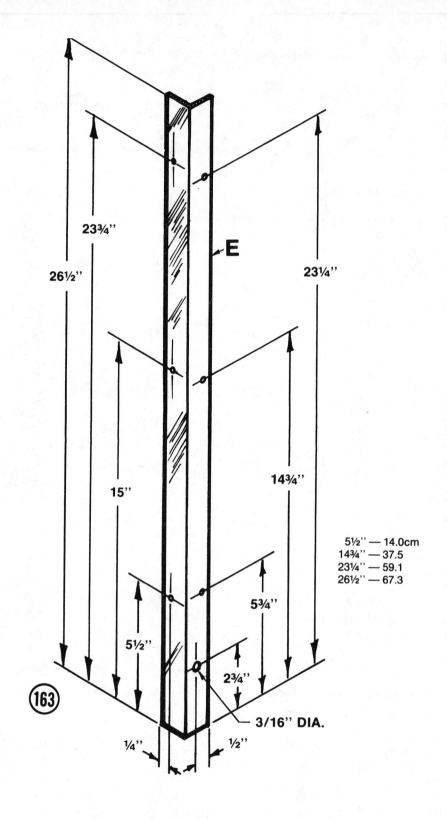

23¾''

26½''

E

23¼''

15''

14¾''

5½'' — 14.0cm
14¾'' — 37.5
23¼'' — 59.1
26½'' — 67.3

5½''

5¾''

2¾''

3/16'' DIA.

¼''

½''

(163)

116

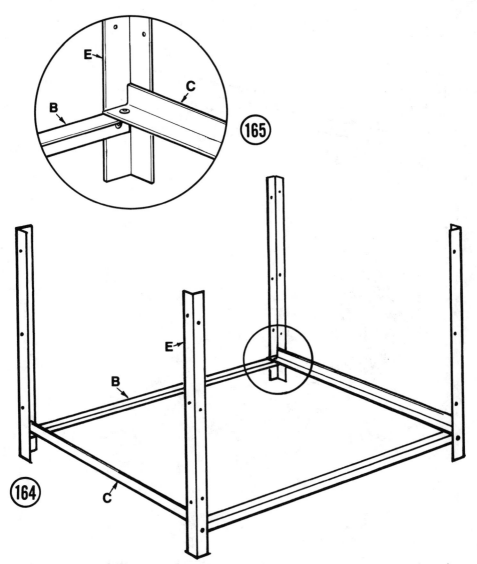

Drill 3/16" holes in four legs E used for cabinet section in position shown, Illus. 163.

Illus. 164 shows assembly of legs for cabinet.

Cross rail B is fastened to E in hole 2¾" up from bottom.

C is cut to length required to butt against inside face of E. C lays on B and is fastened to B in position shown, Illus. 164,165.

117

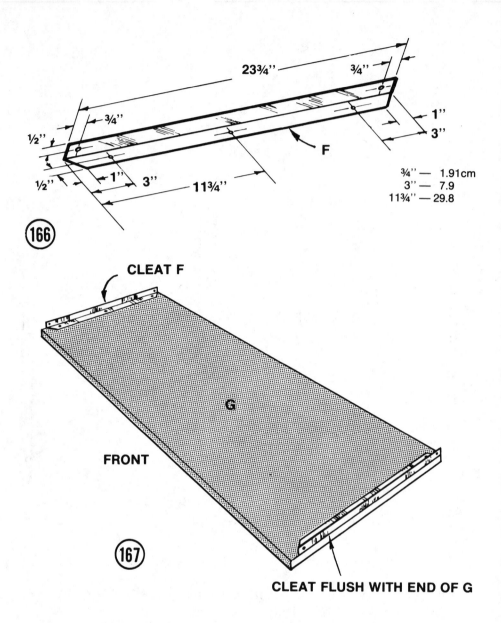

23¾"   ¾"

¾"

½"

1"

3"

½"   1"   3"   11¾"   F

¾" — 1.91cm
3" — 7.9
11¾" — 29.8

(166)

CLEAT F

FRONT

G

(167)

CLEAT FLUSH WITH END OF G

Cut two ¾ x 2'0" x 6'0" plywood or flakeboard surfaced two sides for top G, Illus. 167.

Cut two 1 x 1 x 23¾" angle for F, Illus. 166,167,168,169.

F is fastened flush with end of G. It is recessed ¼" from front edge, Illus. 168, and is flush with back edge, Illus. 169.

118

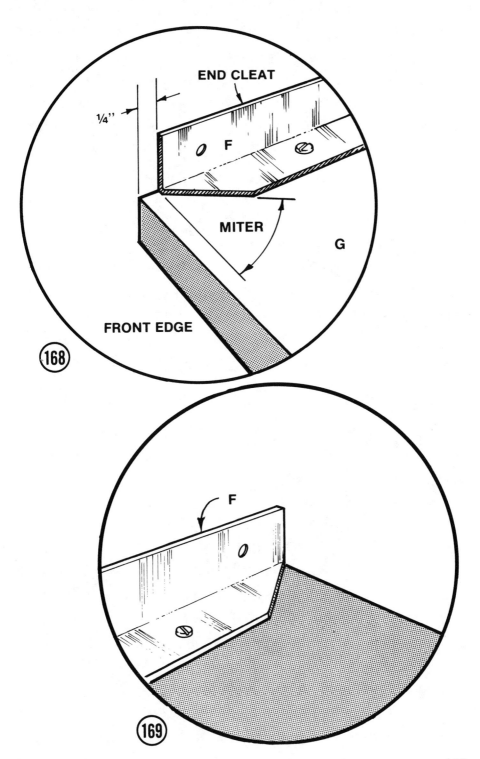

END CLEAT

¼"

F

MITER

G

FRONT EDGE

(168)

F

(169)

119

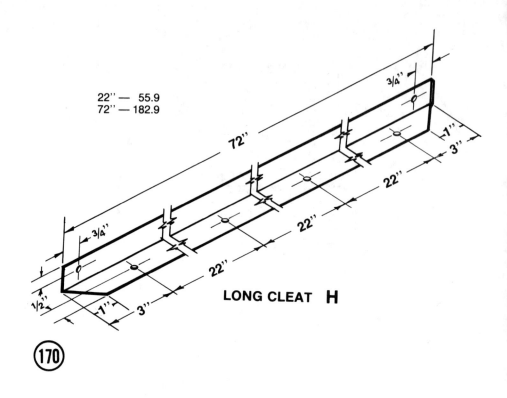

22" — 55.9
72" — 182.9

72"

3/4"

3/4"

22"

22"

22"

1"

3"

3"

1"

1/2"

LONG CLEAT H

(170)

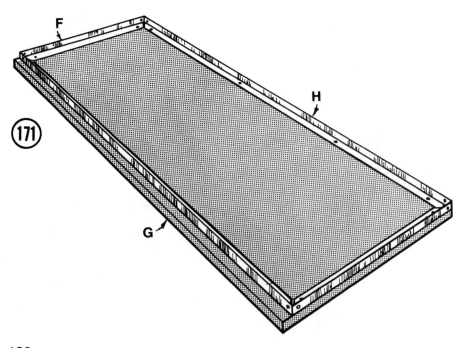

F

H

G

(171)

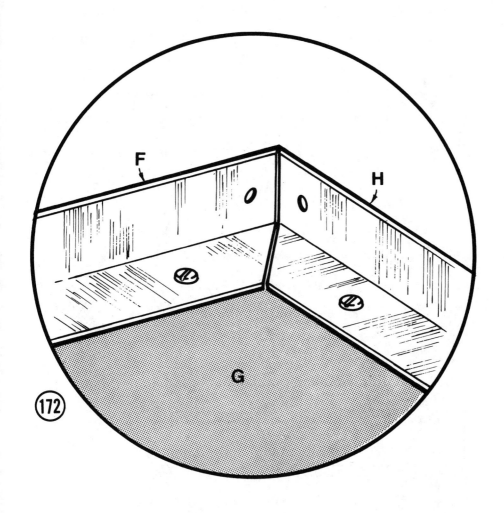

(172)

Cut ends of F to 45° angle shown. Drill 3/16'' holes in position shown.

Fasten F to G using three ¾'' No. 8 aluminum screws. Note position of 3/16'' hole in bottom flange ¾'' from end of F.

Cut two 1 x 1'' angle to length required for H, Illus. 171.

Cut ends to 45° angle. Drill 3/16'' holes in position indicated, Illus. 170, 172.

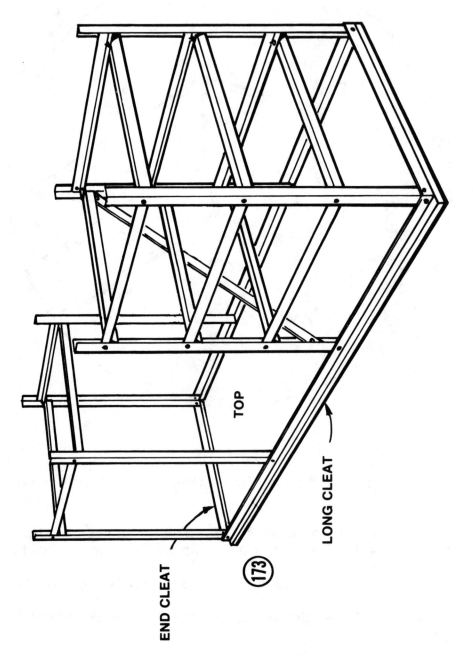

END CLEAR

TOP

⑰

LONG CLEAT

Place assembled drawer framing in position, Illus. 173.

Using holes in F and H, drill holes through legs. Fasten F and H to legs. Bolt F and H to legs using 3/16 x ½'' bolt or ½'' Poprivets.

Place cabinet leg framing in position. Drill holes and temporarily bolt these legs in position with 3/16'' x ¾'' bolts. Place assembled unit in upright position on a level floor to make certain legs are plumb.

Lay assembly on G and remove cabinet leg assembly.

Cut one back K, Illus. 174, from ⅜'' plywood or flakeboard 23⅞ x 23⅛'' or to size framing requires.

Notch bottom corners to receive aluminum framing. Place K in position, Illus.175. Fasten in place using ⅜'' No. 6 panhead tapping screws. Replace 3/16 x ¾'' bolts.

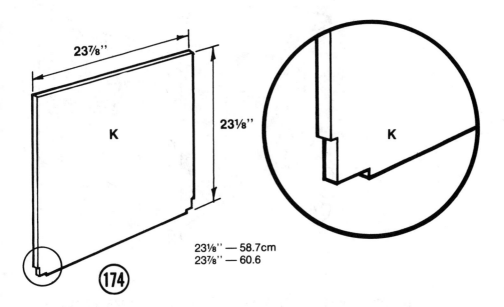

23⅞''

23⅛''

K

K

23⅛'' — 58.7cm
23⅞'' — 60.6

(174)

123

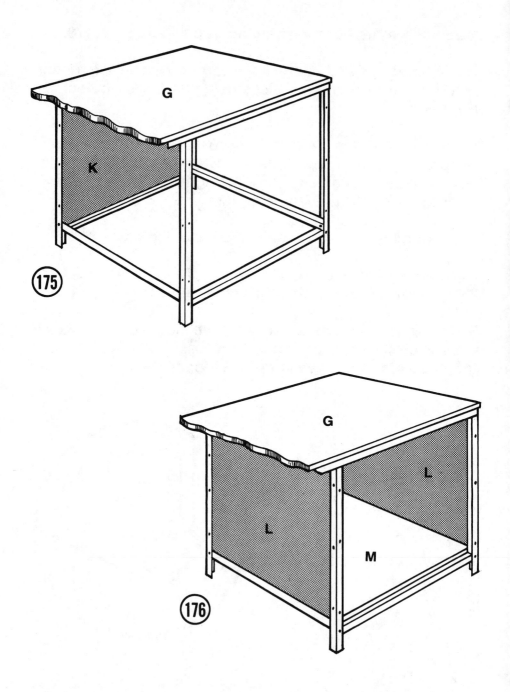

Cut two sides L, Illus. 176, 23⅛ x 23⅛'' or to size required.
Fasten F and H to L with ⅜'' screws. Fasten legs to L with
3/16 x ¾'' bolt.

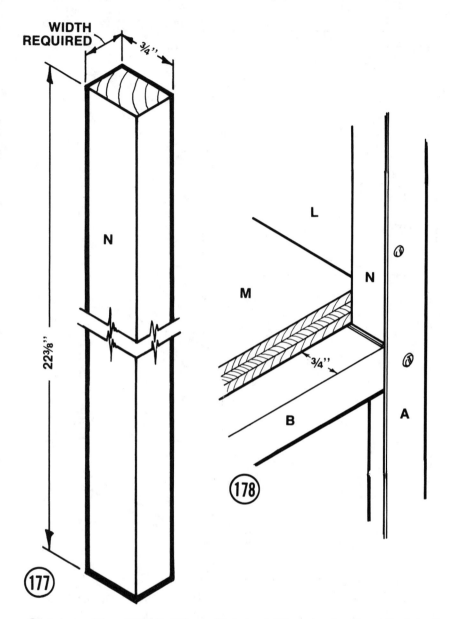

WIDTH REQUIRED

¾"

N

22⅜"

177

L

N

M

¾"

B

A

178

Cut two ¾ x 22⅜" fillers N to width required to finish flush with edge of leg, Illus. 177,178. Fasten leg to N with ⅜" screws.

Cut bottom shelf M from ⅜, ½, ⅝ or ¾" plywood to overall size so M sets ¾" back from face of B. Chisel edge of M if necessary to receive any projecting bolt. Nail through L into M using 1¼" brads.

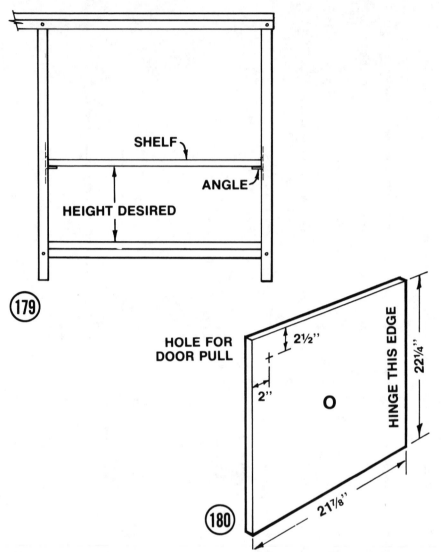

SHELF

ANGLE

HEIGHT DESIRED

(179)

HOLE FOR
DOOR PULL

2½"

2"

O

HINGE THIS EDGE

22¼"

21⅞"

(180)

If an additional shelf is required in cabinet area, cut to size required. Screw 1 x 1" angle to L. Place shelf on angle or sides can be nailed to shelf, Illus. 179.

Cut door O, Illus. 180, from ¾" plywood, 21⅞ x 22¼", or to size opening requires. Drill hole for door pull in upper left hand position. Use bit required for door pull.

Hang door to filler N using 1½" (open size) continuous hinge. Use ¾" No. 4 screws.

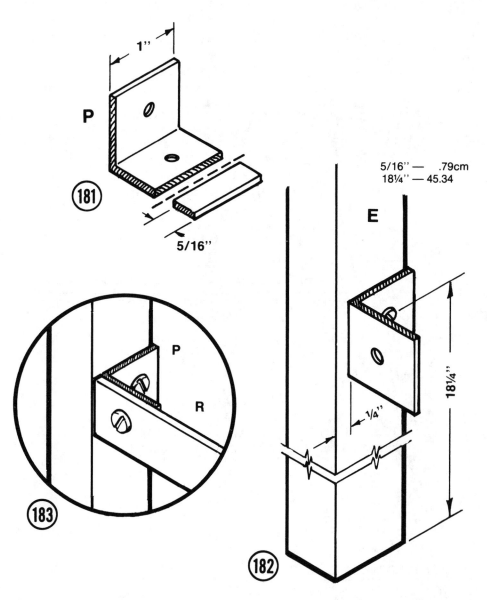

Cut two 1'' pieces of 1 x 1'' angle P, Illus. 181. Cut 5/16'' off.
To reinforce back legs, Illus. 184, fasten P to leg, in position
shown, ¼'' in from outside face, Illus. 182.

Cut ¼ x 1'' aluminum bar stock to length needed for R. Drill
holes in position required.

Bolt or Poprivet R to P, Illus. 183,184.

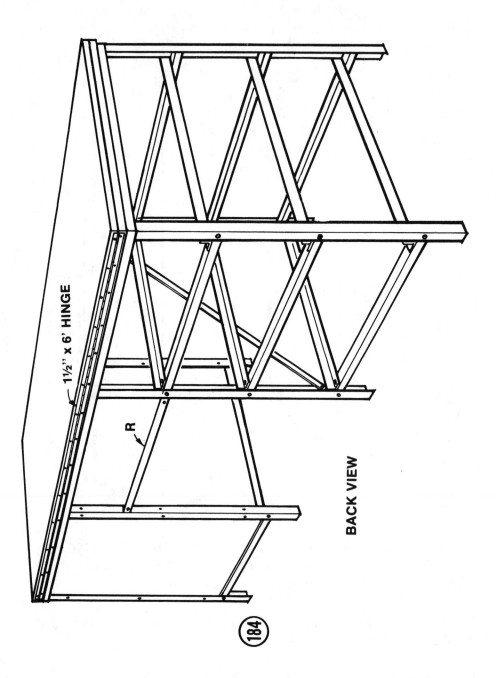

1½" x 6' HINGE

R

BACK VIEW

184

128

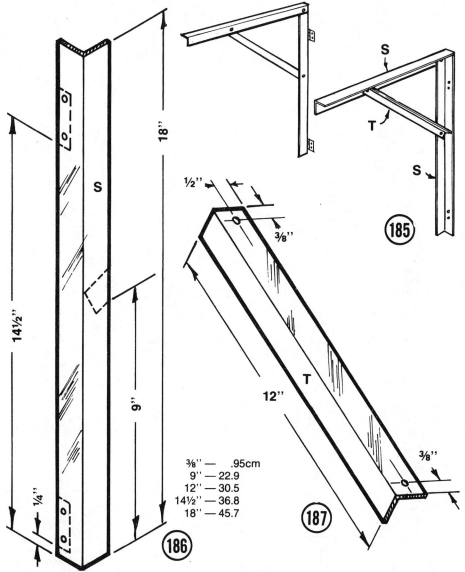

186

185

187

3/8" — .95cm
9" — 22.9
12" — 30.5
14½" — 36.8
18" — 45.7

The two top panels are hinged along back edge with 1½" x 6'0" continuous hinge, Illus. 184. Use ¾" No. 4 screws.

Assemble two table top brackets, Illus. 185. These swing out to support top leaf in open position.

Cut four 1 x 1 x 18" angle for S, Illus. 186.

Cut two 1 x 1 x 12" angle for T, Illus. 187.

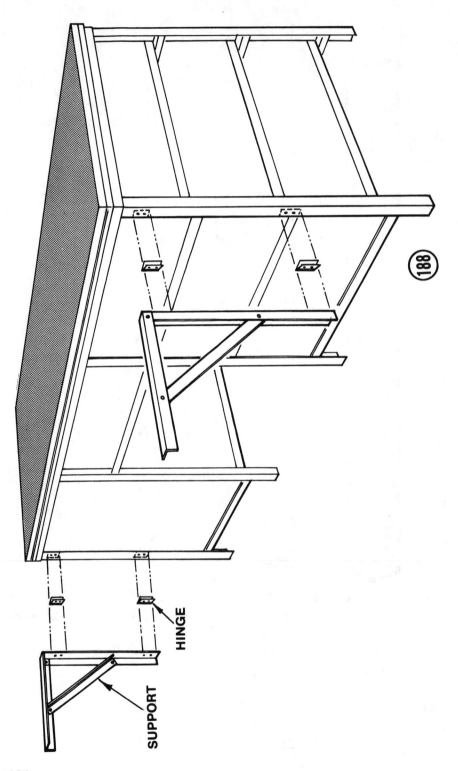

SUPPORT

HINGE

⑱

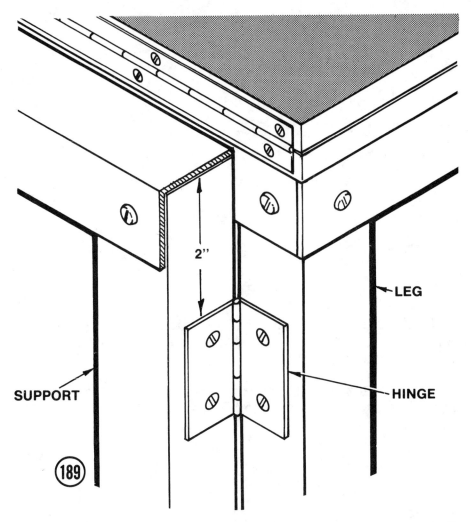

2"

SUPPORT

LEG

HINGE

(189)

Drill 3/16'' holes in position indicated. Bolt or Poprivet S at right angle. Check with 2' square. Bolt or rivet S to T, Illus. 185. Make these brackets in a pair, Illus. 188.

Drill holes in S in position indicated for hinges. Fasten 1½ x 1½'' narrow hinges at height indicated using 3/16 x ½'' stove bolts.

Place bracket against rear outside leg so S is flush with bottom of lower G, Illus. 189. Mark location and drill holes for hinges. Fasten hinge to leg with 3/16 x ¾'' stove bolts in position so it permits brace to fold back.

131

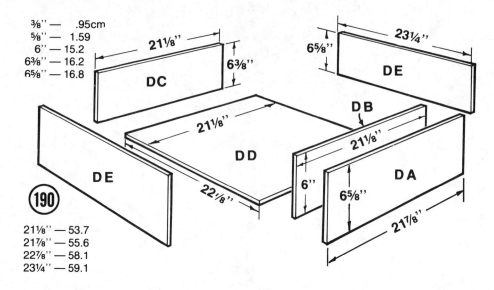

3/8" — .95cm
5/8" — 1.59
6" — 15.2
6 3/8" — 16.2
6 5/8" — 16.8

21 1/8"

6 3/8"

DC

23 1/4"

6 5/8"

DE

DB

21 1/8"

21 1/8"

DD

DE

22 1/8"

DA

6"

6 5/8"

21 7/8"

(190)

21 1/8" — 53.7
21 7/8" — 55.6
22 7/8" — 58.1
23 1/4" — 59.1

Build three drawers using 3/8" plywood. Check width and height of opening between drawer slides to make certain overall dimensions shown, Illus. 190, will fit.

Cut parts to size indicated or size required. Before applying glue, make a dry run. Only brad DC to DD; DD to DB; Illus. 191.

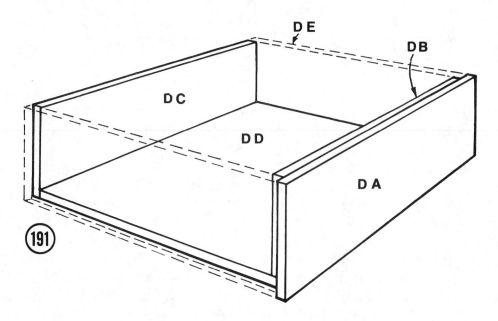

DE

DB

DC

DD

DA

(191)

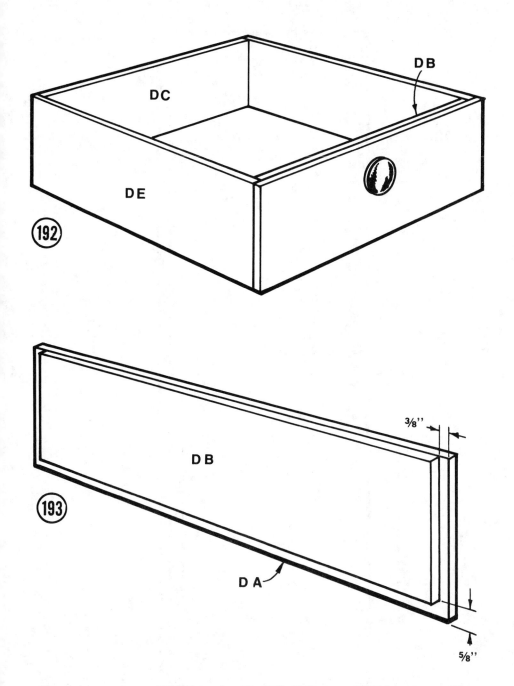

Keeping edge of DE level with DC, DB, brad DE in place, Illus. 192.

Nail DA to DB, Illus. 193.

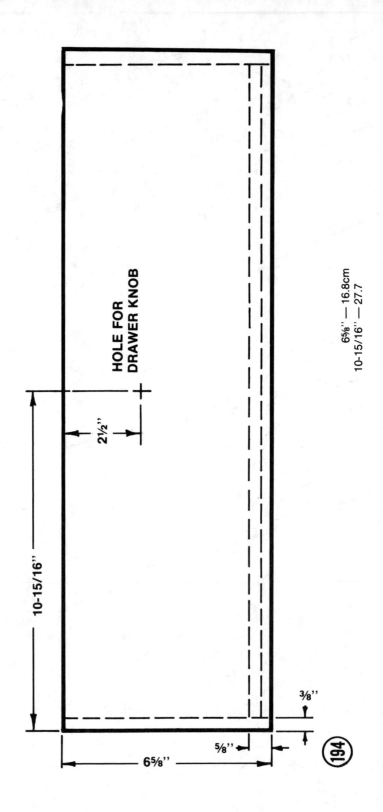

HOLE FOR
DRAWER KNOB

2½"

10-15/16"

6⅝"

⅝"

⅜"

6⅝" — 16.8cm
10-15/16" — 27.7

(194)

134

Drill ⅛" hole through DA, DB in position shown, Illus. 194.

Test drawer in each opening. When OK, take it apart, apply glue and brad parts together. Countersink all brad heads. Apply wood filler.

Fasten 2½" aluminum or dull finished steel drawer knob to each drawer and door.

Apply cabinet catch to door opening following manufacturer's directions.

Fasten ¾" aluminum edging to three exposed edges of G.

With file or emery paper, smooth all corners and angle cuts to eliminate any sharp edges. Place a drop of glue on threads of each exposed bolt. This will insure keeping nuts taut.

Apply paste wax or other finish to plywood surfaces.

Since you will want to keep the unit against a wall when not in use, fasten angle plate casters to all legs. Your aluminum retailer can recommend size available and method of bolting or Popriveting casters to legs.

HOW TO MAKE PICTURE FRAMES

Making professional quality picture frames isn't difficult. It does require a miter box, or miter vise and clamp, Illus. 195, and a 12'' fine back or tenon saw, Illus. 196, with 14 teeth per inch. Smooth miter cuts at 45° angle are essential.

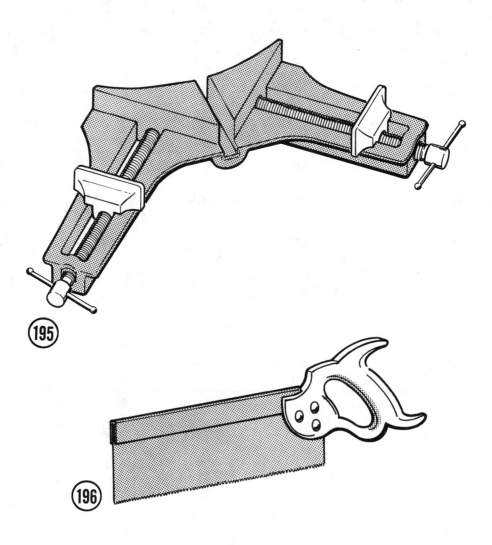

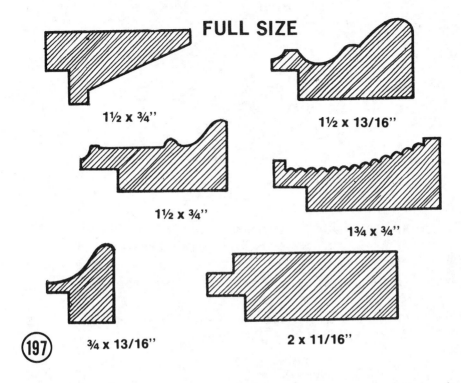

FULL SIZE

1½ x ¾"

1½ x 13/16"

1½ x ¾"

1¾ x ¾"

(197)   ¾ x 13/16"

2 x 11/16"

Making a frame or two as same are needed can be accomplished using one miter vise clamp and time. If you make and use the clamp, Illus. 204, you can make like a pro.

Select the type of picture frame molding you want. Illus. 197 shows a few of the stock moldings readily available in hardware and home centers. These are available in three, four, five and six foot lengths. Always measure overall length on flat side of molding.

To estimate overall length needed, follow this suggestion. If the longest measurement of a picture is more than 8", add 11" to width and height. For example, the picture in Illus. 198 measures 12" wide by 7" high. Since the largest measurement of picture is more than 8", add 11" to width and height. 11" plus 12" equals 23"; 11" plus 7" equals 18". The picture frame should be made 23" wide by 18" high. This permits making a mat to size that complements picture.

137

7" — 17.8
12" — 30.5

12"

7"

(198)

The secret to making a professional quality frame requires cutting 45° miter cuts, one right and one left for each corner. After cutting, place corners together on a level surface to make certain joint fits. Check with a large square.

If miter is off, put both parts back into the miter clamp, Illus. 195, and run the saw through corner, Illus. 199.

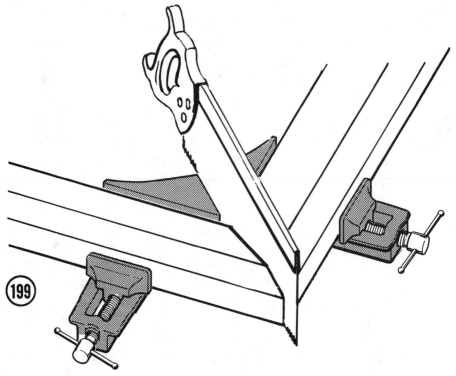

(199)

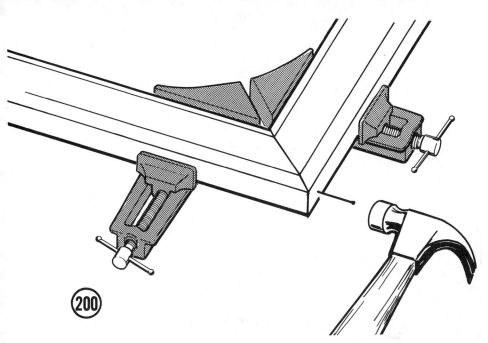

Drill hole to size required prior to driving nail.

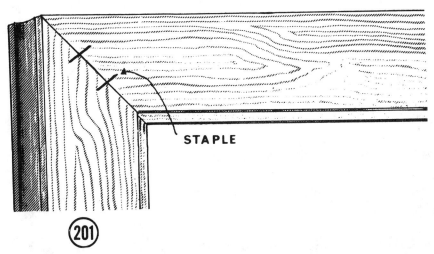

STAPLE

Apply glue to miter. Replace in clamp and drive a finishing nail through joint, Illus. 200. Use length of nail to penetrate at least ½". Countersink head. Allow glue to set time manufacturer specifies. Follow same procedure on each corner.

Those who have a stapling gun find two staples fastened across back, Illus. 201, also help strengthen a miter corner.

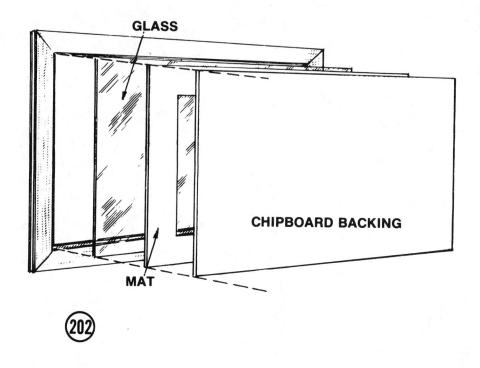

GLASS

CHIPBOARD BACKING

MAT

(202)

Cut glass to size frame requires, Illus. 202.

Art supply stores sell mat boards 32 x 40". Cut mat to size that complements the picture to be framed. Note pictures of comparable size that are suitably framed and cut mat to same width.

After placing glass in frame, place mat, the picture and a cardboard or chipboard backing. Hold backing snugly against picture with 1" brads. Space brads according to need, Illus. 203.

Those framing pictures for office and/or other commercial display frequently use plywood or hardboard with or without a cardboard backing.

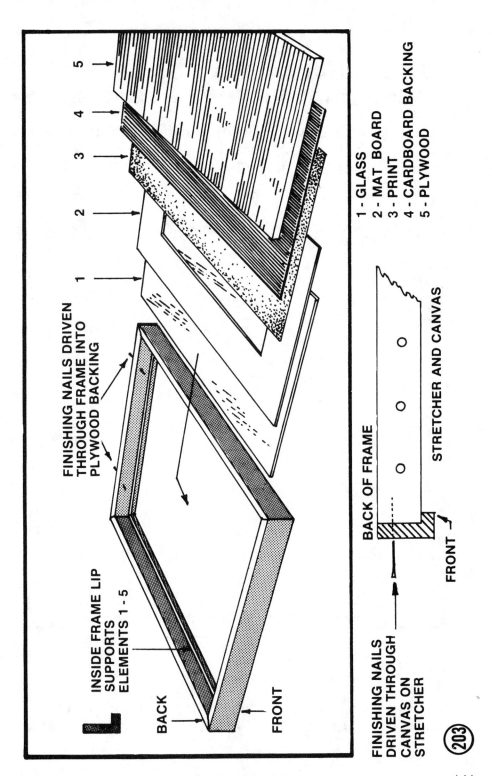

FINISHING NAILS DRIVEN
THROUGH FRAME INTO
PLYWOOD BACKING

INSIDE FRAME LIP
SUPPORTS
ELEMENTS 1 - 5

5
4
3
2
1

1 - GLASS
2 - MAT BOARD
3 - PRINT
4 - CARDBOARD BACKING
5 - PLYWOOD

BACK

FRONT

BACK OF FRAME

STRETCHER AND CANVAS

FRONT

FINISHING NAILS
DRIVEN THROUGH
CANVAS ON
STRETCHER

203

141

HOW TO MAKE A
PROFESSIONAL PICTURE FRAME CLAMP

Those who go into a part or full time business making frames should either buy four corner vise clamps, or better still, make the clamp shown, Illus. 204.

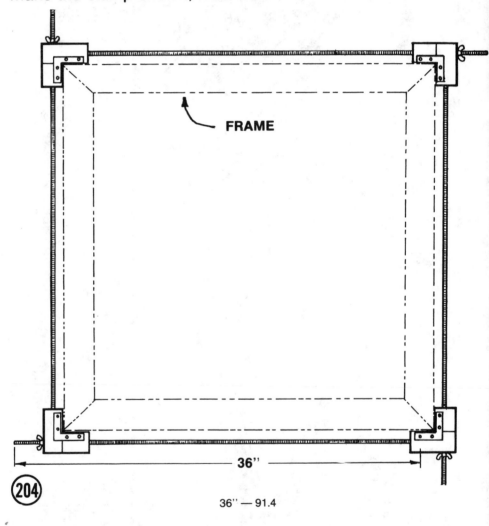

FRAME

(204)

36"

36" — 91.4

When constructed with ¼" x 36" threaded rod, available in hardware stores, the clamp will accommodate frames up to 28".

Those making larger frames should buy 60 or 72" threaded rod.

All material only costs a small fraction of clamps purchased readymade.

LIST OF MATERIAL
4 — ¼ x 36" threaded rod
4 — ½ x 2½ x 2½" flat corner brackets*
4 — wing nuts and washers (for ¼" rod)
1 — 2 x 2 x 24" No. 1 - S4S**

Cut four 2 x 2 x 3½", four 2", Illus. 205. Use a square to draw lines to insure making a square cut. If you have a miter box and backsaw, Illus. 206, it makes perfect cuts.

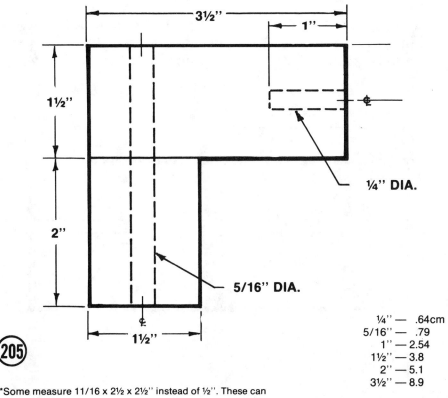

¼" DIA.

5/16" DIA.

(205)

¼"	— .64cm
5/16"	— .79
1"	— 2.54
1½"	— 3.8
2"	— 5.1
3½"	— 8.9

*Some measure 11/16 x 2½ x 2½" instead of ½". These can also be used.

**S4S - Surfaced four sides. Use No. 1 means NO KNOTS.

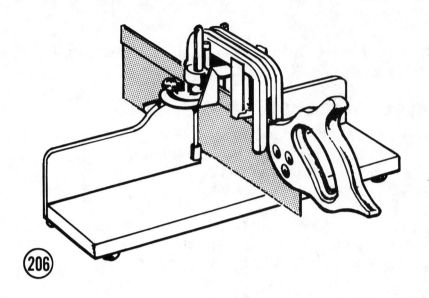

(206)

2 x 2 actually measures 1½ x 1½", note end view, Illus. 207.

Draw diagonals across ends to insure drilling holes in center. Drilling ¼" and 5/16" holes accurately through parts specified is the key to making this clamp.

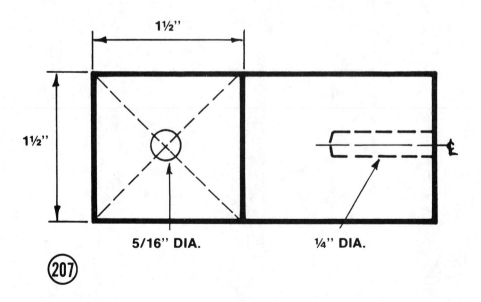

1½"

1½"

5/16" DIA.

¼" DIA.

(207)

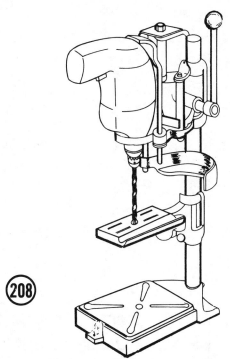

(208)

If you have a drill press or stand for an electric drill, Illus. 208, it helps insure accuracy. If you don't have either, clamp a block of wood to your workbench, Illus. 209. Draw a horizontal line on the block to guide bit.

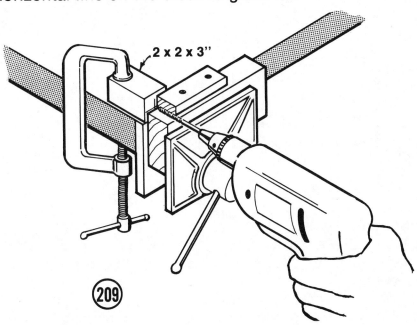

2 x 2 x 3"

(209)

Illus. 205 shows where to drill 5/16" hole clear through, where to drill ¼" hole 1" deep.

Place parts in position DRY — no glue, Illus. 210. Check with square. If OK, fasten corner brace in position.

Remove corner brace, apply glue, dip screws in glue, fasten brace in place. Check corner with a square. Allow glue to set time manufacturer specifies.

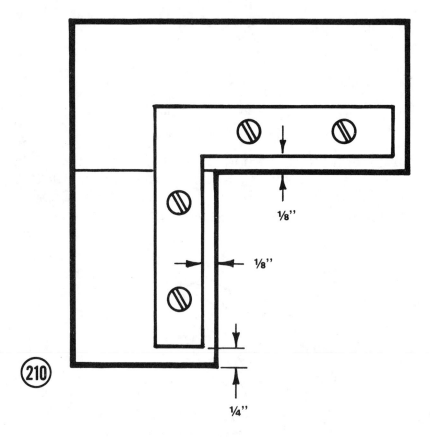

One way to exert even more pressure on corner, after applying glue and brace, apply a nut and washer in position shown, Illus. 211. Tighten nut or wing nut to clamp parts together.

When glue sets up, remove corner, nut and washer.

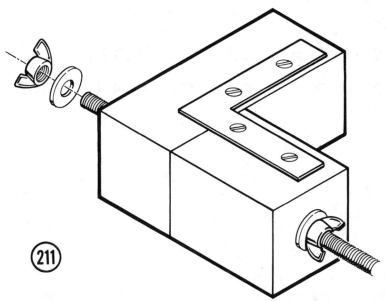

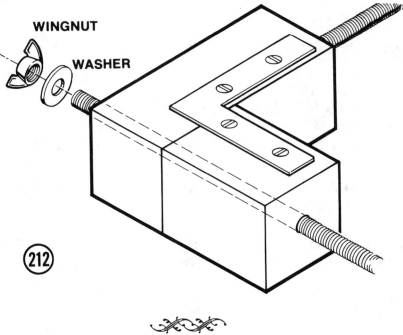

211

Apply glue to 1'' of one end of threaded rod and screw this into ¼'' hole, Illus. 205. When four corners are completed, you have a perfect 90° corner clamp, Illus. 212, that can be adjusted to fit various size frames.

WINGNUT

WASHER

212

HOW TO MAKE A MAT CUTTING GUIDE

This easy to make mat cutter simplifies cutting mats to size desired.

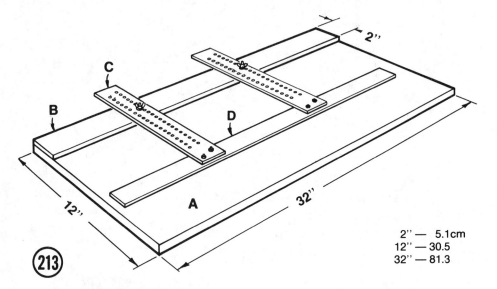

2" — 5.1cm
12" — 30.5
32" — 81.3

LIST OF MATERIAL

1 — ½ x 12 x 32" plywood
1 — ¼ x 2 x 54" plywood
1 — ⅛ x 1 x 30" aluminum bar stock
4 — 3/16 x ¾" machine screws and nuts
2 — 3/16 x 1½" machine screws, wing nuts, washers

Cut base A - ½ x 12 x 32" from plywood or flakeboard. Cut ¼ x 2 x 32" plywood B.

Glue and brad B flush with edge of A. Drill two 3/16" holes through A and B in position shown, Illus. 214, 10" from each end.

Cut two ¼ x 2 x 11" C, Illus. 215.

Drill 3/16" holes in C in position indicated.

148

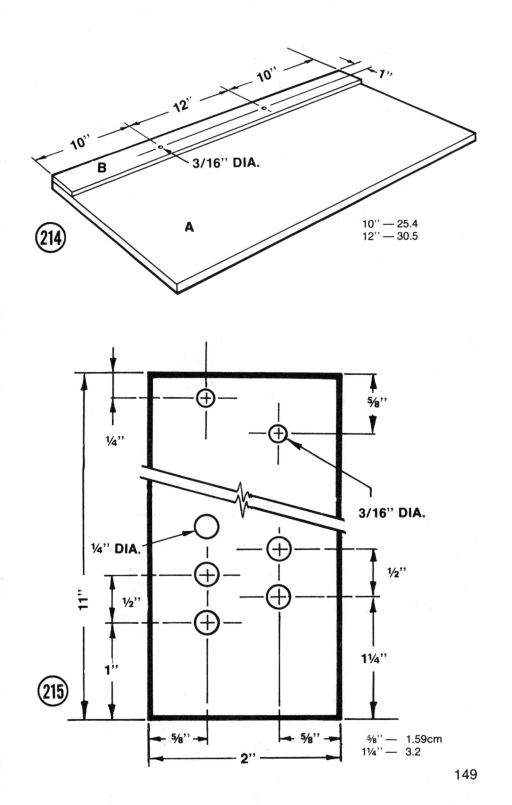

214

10"
12"
10"
1"

3/16" DIA.

B

A

10" — 25.4
12" — 30.5

215

⅝"
¼"
11"
1"
½"
1"

¼" DIA.

3/16" DIA.

½"
1¼"

⅝"
⅝"
2"

⅝" — 1.59cm
1¼" — 3.2

149

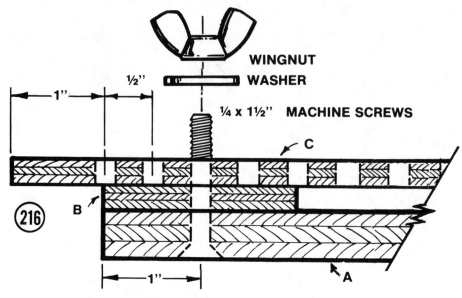

To recess head of 3/16 x 1½" machine screw in bottom of A, Illus. 216, use a countersink bit, Illus. 217.

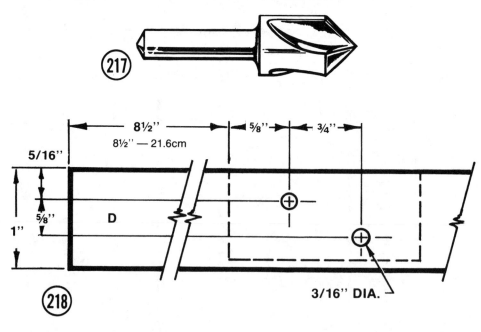

Cut ⅛ x 1 x 30" aluminum bar stock for D. Drill 3/16" holes in position shown, Illus. 218.

Countersink holes in position shown, Illus. 219.

150

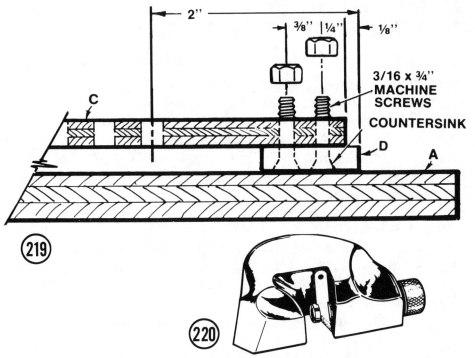

Apply glue to shank of 3/16 x 1½'' machine screw, Illus. 216. Use care not to allow any glue on threads. Insert in position and hold in place with washer and wing nut until glue sets.

Fasten D to C with two 3/16 x ¾'' machine screws and nuts, Illus. 219.

Assemble ABCD as shown, Illus. 213. Check with square.

Slide mat board against straight edge B. Adjust position of C with wing nut on C to obtain desired width of border.

Use a razor blade knife to cut board. Professional straight and bevel cuts can be made with adjustable mat cutter, Illus. 220.

LEARN TO OFFER
WHAT OTHERS WANT TO BUY

The long popular theory that "birds of a feather flock together" is one that also applies to people of every age and economic status, regardless of how or where they live. Those with comparable interests and/or problems invariably gravitate to a state of mind or activity that either provides escape or a solution. This tenet of human behavior influences how we use or misuse our most precious possession — TIME.

Jobs, the life blood of every family and the economic health of a nation, will become increasingly harder to find and hold as industry develops computerized robots. Just as the Japanese have proved their capability of building "recall free" cars through the robotized manufacture of components, so other industries are finding equal success.

No one knows how long they or a company will live and thrive. Learning to shift one's mental gears into new areas of activity will become increasingly more important. Intelligent readers must continuously invest their spare time testing adult capabilities.

Regardless of the years invested putting in an honest day's work, overnight your job could become obsolete. Don't fear this major industrial change. Don't spend breathless nights worrying about that part of your future where you depend on others. Start to rethink your capabilities. Invest spare time, each hour you call your own, developing a skill others want to buy. Learn to create a way of life you presently only dream of living.

Don't become a sucker for a fast buck operator selling a franchise. Even if you find a business you like, DON'T BUY until you have invested at least one year, better yet two, working for the company even if it requires accepting a minimum wage. Actually experience the ups and downs of that business. Forget about losing out by not getting in NOW. Buying a franchise is the fastest way to lose one's life's savings.

Good direction can prove a revelation as to what you can actually accomplish. Learning to do today what you didn't think you could do yesterday is life's way of allowing fate to give you a helping hand. Developing a new area of interest in one's spare time not only helps build self confidence and eliminate fear in the future, but also insures successfully coping with problems as each develops.

Find The Real You. The code word is TRY.

For as long as people live in houses or apartments, trailers or boats, for as long as they consume food, wear clothes and satisfy other needs, your future depends on what you can do. A case in point is making picture frames, replacing wire screening, installing protective services or alarms, and a thousand more areas listed in the cross reference guide. Everyone who makes one picture frame, and enjoys doing it, can find customers in every art adult education class. Satisfy one customer and others hear what you have to offer. Note the number of classified ads offering picture framing in the telephone book. Since you will begin by working out of your present home or apartment, your overhead and selling price per frame can be lower and still profitable. If you successfully cane or replace webbing in one chair, many others will be happy to have you do it – at a cost they can afford.

Every home constantly needs repair, improvement and maintenance. With more people over the age of 65, as compared to those 10 years or younger, millions no longer want to climb a ladder or attempt doing the physical work they formerly did. Easi-Bild Books cover every area of home repair, improvement, even new construction, in words and pictures every reader can easily follow.

TIME is your most precious inheritance. Don't blow it.

INDEX TO MONEY SAVING REPAIRS, IMPROVEMENTS, PATTERNS AND BOOKS
(Number designates Easi-Bild Pattern or Book)

154

155

160

EASI-BILD® LEARN TO EARN BOOKS

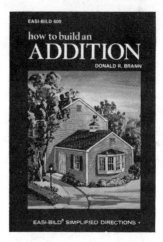

#605 HOW TO INSTALL PANELING

Learn to apply paneling like a pro; build a matching wall to wall storage closet with sliding doors, a fireplace mantel, install valances with indirect lighting, even build a cedar lined storage room. 146pp.,214 illus., plus full size valance patterns simplify every step.

#609 HOW TO BUILD AN ADDITION

Creating additional living space can prove to be one of today's soundest investments. Step-by-step directions explain how to build a 12 x 16', 16 x 24' or any other size one or two story addition, with or without an outside entry. 162pp., 211 illus., simplify every step.

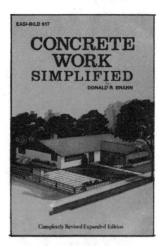

#615 HOW TO MODERNIZE A BASEMENT

Whether you create a family room or turn a basement into an income producing one bedroom apartment with an outside entrance, you will find all the information needed. It explains how to install an outside entry, build stairs, frame partitions, panel walls, lay floor tile and much more. 98pp., 135 illus.

#617 CONCRETE WORK SIMPLIFIED

This book explains everything you need to know to mix concrete, floating, finishing, grooving, edging and pointing, to setting ironwork and anchor bolts. It also explains how to waterproof a basement, install a sump pump, an outside entry and make all kinds of concrete repairs. 194pp., 257 illus.

#823 HOW TO REPAIR, REFINISH, REUPHOLSTER FURNITURE

Apply first aid to ailing furniture and accomplish the work like a pro. Learn to reglue joints, refinish, replace webbing, bent and damaged springs. Want to cane a chair or apply cane webbing? This book tells HOW. Make picture frames, a professional framing clamp and mat cutting board, a quilting frame and rope spring bed. 178pp., 220 illus.

#630 HOW TO BUILD SPORTSMAN'S REVOLVING STORAGE CABINET

Directions simplify building a glass enclosed gun cabinet, wall racks and a 24 x 72'' revolving cabinet that stores everything from guns to clothing. Learn to make what others want to buy. 98pp., 121 illus.

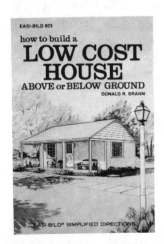

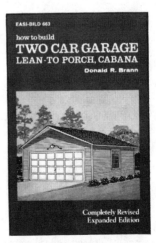

#832 HOW TO BUILD A LOW COST HOUSE

In today's costly housing and energy economy, learning how to build a house you can afford offers great opportunity. In step-by-step directions everyone can follow, this book explains how to build a one bedroom house over a slab; two bedroom house over a full basement, or an earth sheltered three bedroom house. 194pp., 190 illus.

#663 HOW TO BUILD A TWO CAR GARAGE, LEAN-TO PORCH, CABANA

Building a garage can prove to be a richly rewarding experience. Letters from readers who built this garage confirm the task altered their outlook on life. Many who build turn it into an income producing singles apartment. 130pp., 142 illus.

#668 BRICKLAYING SIMPLIFIED

All who seek income, peace of mind, an economical solution to a costly problem or employment in a trade where opportunity is unlimited, find this book a real guide to better living. It explains how to lay bricks, a wall, walk, veneer a house, build a barbecue, etc. It turns amateurs into pros. 146pp., 212 illus.

#669 HOW TO BUILD BIRDHOUSES AND BIRD FEEDERS

Encouraging a child to build feeders and birdhouses can stimulate a lifetime interest in woodworking. Full size patterns not only simplify building but also insure success. Helping a child turn a piece of wood into a useable and saleable article builds instant self confidence. 66pp., 86 illus.

#672 HOW TO BUILD WORKBENCHES AND SAWHORSE TOOLCHEST

To economically solve costly repairs and improvements, every home, apartment and place of business needs a workbench. This encourages those who build one to build others for resale. Simplified directions show how to build 6' workbenches, with a 6' vise on one or both sides, big drawers and tool compartments, to foldaway wall benches that require a minimum of floor space. 180pp., 250 illus., plus a full size foldout pattern.

#674 HOW TO INSTALL A FIREPLACE

Everyone who wants to install a woodburning stove, build a brick fireplace or install a prefabricated metal fireplace and chimney, will find all the direction they need. Installing a chimney completely within or recessed flush with an outside wall is clearly explained and illustrated. 242pp., 354 illus.

170

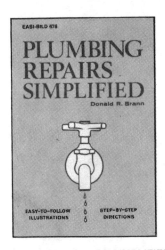

#675 PLUMBING REPAIRS SIMPLIFIED

Homeowners who dislike having their budget and peace of mind destroyed by a faulty plumbing fixture find this book helps save time, temper and money. Everyone who has learned to bake a cake or drive a car can easily replace parts and make repairs like a pro. Read, learn, then do what directions suggest and see how much more living you get out of life. 194pp., 820 illus.

#679 HOW TO BUILD A STABLE AND RED BARN TOOL HOUSE

Measuring 20 x 30', this three box stall stable is easy to build while it makes a dream come true. Every step of construction, from having a reason to build (to create an individual and not a joiner), selecting a site, to building the cupola, is explained, illustrated and simplified. Directions also simplify building an 8 x 10' or larger red barn tool house. 178pp., 197 illus.

#680 HOW TO BUILD A ONE CAR GARAGE, CARPORT, CONVERT A GARAGE INTO A STABLE

Building a one car garage with ample space for a workshop, or turning a one car garage into a two box stall stable is clearly explained. Directions tell how to raise a garage to obtain needed headroom, build a carport, lean-to toolhouse and a cupola. 146pp., 181 illus.

#682 HOW TO ADD AN EXTRA BATHROOM

This complete, easy to read guide to home plumbing helps make a dream come true for only the cost of fixtures. In easy to follow directions, it tells how to make the installation and save a bundle. Those who don't want to do any plumbing discover sizeable savings can be effected by preparing the area, then having a plumber make the installation. Read, learn, save. 162pp., 200 illus.

#683 CARPETING SIMPLIFIED

Laying carpet in your home can provide the experience needed to do the same work for others. This book explains how a pro performs each step in words and pictures every reader can easily follow. Every type of carpeting, over any kind of floor, with or without padding, is explained, illustrated and simplified. Directions explain how to carpet stairs, install protective under the carpet electronic alarm mats, and much, much more. 178pp., 223 illus.

#684 HOW TO TRANSFORM A GARAGE INTO LIVING SPACE

Transforming a garage into a living-bedroom, with a kitchen and bathroom, can provide a safe and economical solution to a costly nursing home problem. It can also become an important income producer. Step-by-step directions assume the reader has never done any of this work and explains every step. 130pp., 139 illus.

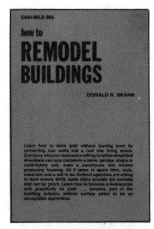

#685 HOW TO REMODEL BUILDINGS

With abandoned big city housing units available to all who are willing to rehabilitate and occupy same, this book explains how tenants can become landlords with only an investment of time and effort. It tells how to turn an abandoned multi-family building, store, garage or warehouse into rentable housing. Every step explained and illustrated. Read and learn how to become a homeowner without spending a lot of money. 258pp., 345 illus.

#690 HOW TO BUILD BARS

Building a bar offers a fun way to furnish a recreation room. Learning to build a straight, L-shaped or any of the seven bars described provides an easy way to start a part or full time business. Doing something today you didn't know how to do yesterday broadens one's sphere of activity. 162pp., 195 illus.

#694 ELECTRICAL REPAIRS SIMPLIFIED

Learning to make electrical repairs requires reading, noting location of each part shown in step-by-step illustrations, then doing what directions specify. This book takes the fear, mystery and inflated cost out of many troublesome repairs. Knowing what circuit controls each fixture or outlet that requires repair provides the safety and peace of mind this job requires. A special feature even explains how to install wiring in a dollhouse. 134pp., 224 illus.

#695 HOW TO INSTALL
PROTECTIVE ALARM DEVICES

Recapture peace of mind by securely protecting all doors and windows with professional alarm devices. Learn how to discourage a break-in with magnetic contacts that automatically trigger a telephone dialer to the police, sound a loud alarm bell, instantly detect movement with easy to install radar. A layman's guide to professionally installed electronic protection. 130pp., 146 illus.

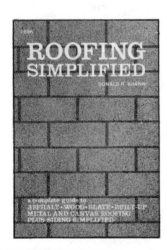

#696 ROOFING SIMPLIFIED

This "business of your own" book turns amateurs into professional roofers. Learn to repair or replace an asphalt, wood or slate roof; apply roll roofing, make a roofer's safety harness, walk and work on a roof with no fear of falling, plus much more. 130pp., 168 illus.

#697 FORMS, FOOTINGS, FOUNDATIONS, FRAMING, STAIR BUILDING

This book tells every reader how to get into the building industry. Whether you build your own house, buy a prefab or want a career in building, this book tells everything you need to know about forms, footings, foundations, framing and stair building. 210pp., 310 illus.

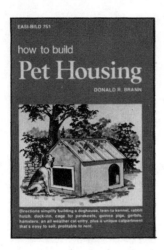

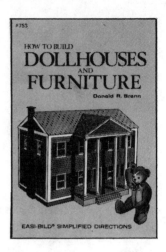

#751 HOW TO BUILD PET HOUSING

Encourage all who love pets to build the shelter each needs. Learn how to build a doghouse, lean-to kennel, rabbit hutch, duck-inn, parakeet cage, an all weather cat entry, plus a unique catpartment that's easy to sell, easy to rent. 178pp., 252 illus.

#753 HOW TO BUILD DOLLHOUSES & FURNITURE

To create a memory a little girl will never forget, build one of the three dollhouses offered in this book. Those searching for a part or full time money making hobby find a ready market for dollhouses. Full size patterns simplify making fourteen pieces of dollhouse furniture. 194pp., 316 illus.

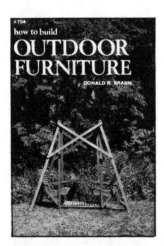

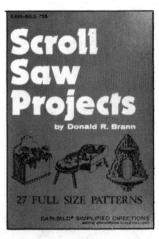

#754 HOW TO BUILD OUTDOOR FURNITURE

Easy to follow step-by-step directions, plus a big foldout full size pattern, simplify tracing and cutting all parts to exact shape required. Learn how to build curved back lawn chairs, a matching settee, four passenger lawn glider, a chaise on wheels and much, much more. 130pp., 174 illus, plus full size pattern.

#756 SCROLL SAW PROJECTS

Helping everyone, a child or retiree, successfully turn a piece of wood into a handsome, useable and saleable article, builds the ego. This book insures success. 27 full size patterns permit tracing all parts, then assembling each in exact position shown on pattern. 130pp., 146 illus.

174

#757 HOW TO BUILD A KAYAK
Simplified directions and full size frame patterns permit building this extremely light yet sturdy kayak to three different lengths, 14'3", 16'9", or 18'0". It can easily be carried on a cartop rack and used by one or two adults. Patterns insure cutting each frame to exact size required. This book includes full size patterns for all frames.

#758 HOW TO MODERNIZE A KITCHEN, BUILD BASE AND WALL CABINETS, POLE TYPE FURNITURE
Of special interest to every homeowner who appreciates the convenience and long term Capital Gains of a completely modernized kitchen. 210pp., 263 illus.

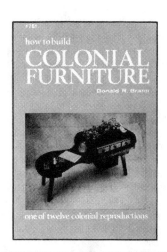

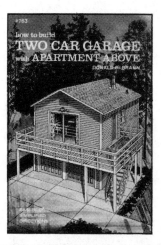

#761 HOW TO BUILD COLONIAL FURNITURE
Building colonial reproductions can provide hours of complete escape. You not only obtain furniture at a fraction of retail cost, but also enjoy every hour. Easy to follow directions and full size patterns simplify building a cobbler's bench, hutch cabinet, blanket chest, under the eaves rope bed, wall cabinet and other useful pieces. 12 colonial reproductions are offered. 258pp., 342 illus.

#763 HOW TO BUILD A TWO CAR GARAGE WITH APARTMENT ABOVE
All who seek an economical solution to a costly housing problem should read this book. It explains how to build a two car, two story garage. Directions also explain how to add a second story apartment to an existing garage. Space above provides a living, bedroom, kitchen and bathroom. Ideal for a single or couple. 194pp., 226 illus.

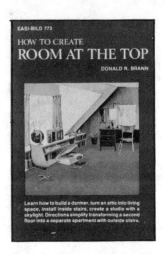

#771 TOYMAKING AND CHILDREN'S FURNITURE SIMPLIFIED

As every reader soon discovers, toymaking possesses a certain magic. Turning a piece of lumber into a whimsical rocking horse with a personality captures a child's imagination, triggers an interest in woodworking long before they have any idea how it was made. This book simplifies building 17 different toys and children's furniture. 194pp., 330 illus., plus a big foldout full size pattern.

#773 HOW TO CREATE ROOM AT THE TOP

Need more living space or a complete apartment with outside stairs? This book tells how to raise a roof with an easy to build dormer, install a skylight for those seeking a studio apartment, create rental living space at low cost. Transforming an extra bedroom and/or attic that can be reached with outside stairs insures privacy. 162pp., 239 illus.

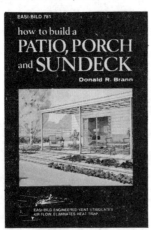

#781 HOW TO BUILD A PATIO, PORCH AND SUNDECK

Simplified directions take all the inflated cost out of building a front or back porch, a patio to length and width specified or to size desired, a carport and sundeck. Every step, from laying footings to installation of railings, is illustrated. Directions also explain how to make screens, porch repairs, swimming pool enclosure and much more. 146pp., 220 illus.

#792 HOW TO BUILD COLLECTORS' DISPLAY CASES

Learn to build handsome, clear acrylic, museum quality, floor, table top and wall display cabinets. These provide the perfect way to display every kind of possession from dolls, china, figurines, etc. Retailers buy these cases for store use as readily as for resale. 194pp., 229 illus.

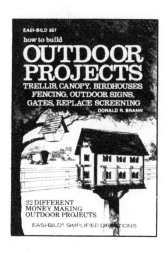

#804 HOW TO BUILD WALL TO WALL BOOKCASES AND STEREO CABINETS

Directions explain how to build free standing cabinets for those who rent, built-ins for those who own. By using the moldings specified, a truly professional job can be done. For those who enjoy stereo, directions simplify building wall to wall cabinets from floor to ceiling, a Lo Boy, High Boy, also a handsome record cabinet. 194pp., 232 illus.

#807 HOW TO BUILD OUTDOOR PROJECTS

This book explains how to build handsome colonial style fencing, birdhouses and feeders, a trellis, over the door canopy with or without side enclosures. Learn how to replace screening and much, much more. 20 different money making projects are explained and simplified. The ideal book for those seeking to earn extra income. 210pp., 239 illus.

#811 HOW TO BUILD GREENHOUSES — WALK-IN, WINDOW, SUNHOUSE, GARDEN TOOL HOUSE

Of special interest to everyone who enjoys the fun and relaxation of growing plants the year round. The sunhouse appeals to sun lovers who enjoy winter sunbathing. 210pp., 229 illus.

#816 HOW TO LAY CERAMIC TILE

In simplified, step-by-step directions, this book explains how to apply ceramic and quarry tile to walls, floors, countertops and patios. A LEARN TO EARN book that turns amateurs into pros. 178pp., 225 illus.

#850 HOW TO FIND A JOB, START A BUSINESS

With record unemployment and those receiving welfare, pension or Social Security benefits reaching new highs, the economic future of a nation depends on the creation of meaningful jobs. This book encourages every reader from teenagers, retirees to executives living under too much stress to turn time into a business of their own with no capital investment other than for material and tools. It explains how to offer what others want to buy without being taken to the cleaners buying a franchise operation. 210pp., 304 illus., explain how everyone interested can create a profitable business.

#600 COMPLETE EASI-BILD CATALOG

Anybody can do anything if they follow directions offered in Easi-Bild Books and Full Size Patterns. The catalog illustrates hundreds of patterns and home repair and improvement books. Give this book to a youth searching to find a career and many will soon be building everything from furniture, boats, garages to houses. Getting experience in their own home encourages doing the same work for others.